# THE COTTON INDUSTRY

## IN

## HOLLINGWORTH

## AND

## MOTTRAM-IN-LONGDENDALE

# The Cotton Industry
# in
# Hollingworth
# and
# Mottram-in-Longdendale

## by Ian Haynes

£4.25

# THE COTTON INDUSTRY

# IN

# HOLLINGWORTH

# AND

# MOTTRAM-IN-LONGDENDALE

## by

## Ian Haynes

Published by Ian Haynes 2008

Printed and published in 2008 by
Ian Haynes 18 Nook Lane Ashton-under-Lyne Lancashire England


Text © Ian Haynes 2008


ISBN 978-0-9542171-3- 6

**By the same author**

*Cotton in Ashton* (Libraries and Arts Committee, Tameside Metropolitan Borough 1987)
ISBN 978-0-904506-14-3

*Stalybridge Cotton Mills* (Neil Richardson 1990)
ISBN 978-1-85216-054-8 .

*Dukinfield Cotton Mills* (Neil Richardson 1993)
ISBN 978-1-85216-080-7

*Mossley Textile Mills* (Neil Richardson 1996)
ISBN 978-1-85216-109-5

*History of the Cotton Industry in Droylsden, with Audenshaw and Denton* (Ian Haynes 2004)
ISBN 978-0-9542171-1-2

*Hyde Cotton Mills* 2nd Edition (Ian Haynes 2005)
ISBN 978-0-9542171-2-9

**Acknowledgements**
I am grateful to the following for their help with research and illustrations:-the staffs of
Cheshire Record Office, Glossop Library, Local Studies Library, Matlock, Manchester Central
Library and Tameside Local Studies Library.
Also, Chris Aspin, Joan Bone, Mary Jessop, Mike Nevell and Peter Solar.

# Introduction

By the latter part of the eighteenth century until well into the twentieth century the cotton industry played a vital part in the economy of the Hollingworth and Mottram-in-Longdendale (hereafter simply referred to as Mottram) district and in the working lives of a large proportion of the population. In the following pages will be found a history of the development of the cotton industry in the area during that period followed by individual histories of all of the known cotton mills and finishing works.

Hollingworth and Mottram were separately administered for civil purposes until the 1930s. The centuries old Cheshire townships lay contiguous to each other in the westernmost part of the Longdendale Valley on the right bank of the River Etherow, divided from each other by an irregular boundary that followed no obvious physical features. Local Boards of Health were formed at Hollingworth in 1871 and at Mottram two years later and then, from 1894, both places were run by urban district councils. It was in 1936 that their close association was recognised officially with the creation of Longdendale UDC to govern both places. The newly formed administrative unit also included part of the civil parish of Hattersley, which was of some significance to the subject of this history as the additional area included the sites of two early cotton mills. Longdendale UDC ceased to exist on the formation of Tameside Metropolitan Borough following the local government re-organisation of 1974; it corresponded more or less with the present Longdendale ward of Tameside MB. The area is bounded to the south and east by the River Etherow, which also forms the boundary with Derbyshire, and by the course of one of its tributary streams, Hollingworth Brook. To the north lies Pennine moorland rising to over 1,300 feet above sea level and the area is bounded on the west by the towns of Hyde and Stalybridge. The district is a maximum of about two miles wide east to west and three miles north to south and covers an area of just under four square miles. Manchester city centre lies about nine miles to the west and Glossop about two and a half miles to the south east.

The topography of the Hollingworth and Mottram district is predominantly hilly and it is one of the least built-up parts of Tameside, with a population density only half that of Tameside as a whole. As recently as 1961 the population stood at just 4,626 but extensive residential development in the following decade enabled the population to more than double by 1971. The population has gradually declined over the last 30 years or so and at the time of the 2001 census stood at 9,733.

Two local views from J Aikin *Description of the Country Thirty to Forty Miles Round Manchester* (1795).

Upper: Mottram village

Lower: Broadbottom Bridge. The building in the background is
Besthill Mill, on the Derbyshire side of the River Etherow.

# The Rise and Fall
# of the
# Local Cotton Industry

By the 1780s, when cotton mills are first recorded, the Hollingworth and Mottram area already had a long association with textile production. The working of wool, flax and hemp and other materials, including cotton to a small extent, is recorded in the seventeenth century. There are indications that before 1700 woollen production had gained pre-eminence and the local industry was sufficiently important to merit the establishment of at least one fulling mill by 1763, turned by the waters of the River Etherow, at Hodge, in the south of the district. In a trade directory of 1781 half a dozen woollen manufacturers are listed with abodes at Mottram, who were standing the Manchester market. Very soon, however, the dominance of the woollen industry was to be lost to its rival, the rapidly expanding cotton industry.

The cotton industry started its great expansion early in the eighteenth century as the demand for light textiles increased. Initially, this increased demand could be met by expanding the existing domestically based industry but there eventually came a point where demand could no longer be met. The yarn production of the hand spinners with their single wheels could not keep pace with the consumption

of yarn by the hand loom weavers. The solution to this problem arrived with the invention of machines that could produce cotton yarn at a vastly faster rate than could the cottage wheel. Hargreaves' spinning jenny, introduced in 1767, was a small, light machine that could be worked by hand and which did not greatly disrupt the existing domestic system of production. The jenny, however, could only produce yarn suitable for use as weft and the problem was not solved until the introduction of Arkwright's water frame for the spinning of warp yarns in 1769. It was the water frame and its attendant machines that led to the first great revolution in the organisation of the cotton industry. The Arkwright system of cotton spinning required relatively large amounts of motive power such as could be supplied by water, via a water wheel. The best way of supplying such motive power to the newly invented machinery was by collecting the machines together in large, often purpose-built structures and the first viable water powered cotton spinning mills, starting with Arkwright's mill at Cromford, Derbyshire, in 1771, came into existence.

Once Arkwright's system of cotton spinning became known there was no shortage of men keen to invest in new mills, either in

adapted buildings or purpose-built ones, particularly after Arkwright's patent for spinning by rollers was withdrawn in 1781. Water power sites, even on small streams, were much sought after. Areas such as Longdendale, with the River Etherow and its numerous tributary streams with large falls of water, were magnets for investors in cotton mills.

A valuation of Hollingworth of 1788[1] reveals that by that date the township contained seven cotton mills, with an eighth under construction. Four of the sites are known to have used water power and it is likely that the others also did. Clearly the largest of the seven mills that were in operation, judging by the amount of the valuation, was Hollingworth Mill, built about 1785 by Thomas Cardwell by the side of the River Etherow, for cotton spinning on the Arkwright system. William Kelsall's mill was in existence by 1786 and the mill in course of erection was Wood's, on land acquired for the purpose in 1786. Nothing is known of the other mills prior to the 1788 valuation and it is possible that some or all of them pre-dated Cardwell's. One mill, belonging to James Harrop, is stated to have been used only for carding, a preparatory process prior to spinning, but the rest probably also did spinning. It was quite common for small, early

*Part of Stockdale's map published in 1794. Millbrook Mill (Sidebottom's Factory), Arrowscroft Mill (Cardwell's Factory) and Hill End Mill (Lowe's Factory) are indicated.*

mills, such as those at Hollingworth, to use water power only for the preparation machinery while spinning was done on hand powered machines. However, if spinning was being carried out by water power it must have been on the Arkwright system, as at Cardwell's mill.

Another potential Arkwright-type mill was built at Hollingworth, at Arrowscroft, in 1789, by Thomas Cardwell and mention should also be made here of Millbrook Mill, erected in the same year. The original part of the latter mill stood on the Tintwistle side of Hollingworth Brook but in later years the majority of the buildings were erected on the

Hollingworth side. In the early 1830s the machine maker Joseph Shepley gave evidence to the Factories Enquiry Commission respecting his time spent working as a child at Millbrook Mill[2]. He commenced working there about 1792, at the age of six years, as a scavenger, recovering cotton from underneath and around the machinery. After a year he progressed to the job of piecer, joining the broken ends of yarn on spinning machines, which he did for a further 10 years before becoming a spinner. As a child Shepley's hours of work were from 6 am until 7 pm, with one hour allowed for dinner. No allowance was made for breakfast

or tea but he did have the opportunity to go out of the mill to the side of the brook for five or ten minutes about four times a day. About 60 children, both boys and girls, were employed at the mill, their ages ranging mainly from eight to fifteen or sixteen years, with a few as young as six. Despite the long hours, completely unregulated by legislation at that period, Shepley managed to find the energy to attend night school three times a week, as well as Sunday school.

No potential Arkwright-type cotton spinning mills are known in Mottram township, where water power sites were in much shorter supply, prior to the mid 1790s. The woollen mill at Hodge, in the Broadbottom district of the township, was converted into a cotton mill by one Neddy Holt about 1787. He installed machinery for the preparatory processes of carding and roving. This mill seems to have been complementary to one that Holt built at about the same time, known as Clough Mill. This mill was located on the Hattersley side of Hurst Clough Brook in the part of Hattersley township that much later became a part of Longdendale Urban District. Clough Mill contained machinery for processes subsequent to cotton spinning, such as winding and warping the yarn ready for weaving.

The next revolution in cotton spinning after Arkwright's water frame came with the invention of the spinning mule by Samuel Crompton in 1779. The mule, as the name suggests, was a cross between the water frame and the jenny, the outcome of which was a machine that could spin both warp and weft yarn to almost any degree of fineness. It opened up whole new markets for British cotton manufacturers who could now compete with imported cotton goods, such as Indian muslins. For some time the mule remained wholly hand operated due to the complexity of its motions. However, it soon grew to a size that was not practicable for use in cottages and mule spinning workshops were set up in all sorts of accommodation; in barns and other outbuildings, in garrets and in purpose-built premises. The mule did not immediately supplant the jenny and the water frame and the three modes of spinning were carried on in parallel for many years. It was only in the new industry of fine cotton spinning that the mule dominated from the start.

As already mentioned, hand operated spinning machines, whether mule frames or jennies, were often housed in small factories along with powered machinery such as carding machines. The source of motive power was not necessarily water, for machines such as carding engines did not demand the regularity of motion, like that provided by a water wheel, that cotton spinning did. Horse wheels were commonly adopted for turning machinery and Aikin in 1795 specifically mentions that form of motive power being in use at Mottram[3]. These horse powered workshops or small factories did not need to be located close to a stream and they were often to be found in the centres of towns and villages.

At Mottram, John Wagstaffe, in 1786, converted a barn for use as a rudimentary sort of cotton mill and later, about the mid 1790s, he started a similar, but purpose-built, concern nearby. Unfortunately we know nothing of the machinery that Wagstaffe was employing or whether it was turned by hand or horse power or a mixture of the two. There was no stream in the vicinity and the name 'Dry Mill' applied to the later building confirms the ab-sence of water power. It seems likely that the cotton mill at Rough Field, Mottram, was a similar type of concern to Wagstaffe's. When the premises were put up for sale in 1793 they were described as 'house and factory adjoining' and the location does not seem to have had the potential for water power. Both of these early factories had fallen into disuse by 1815.

It was not until 1790 that water power was successfully applied to the rather complicated, discontinuous movements of the spinning mule, rendering it into a semi-automatic machine. Henceforth, cotton mills started to be set up for spinning by means of powered mule frames. The old hand operated mules rapidly became obsolete, except perhaps for the spinning of the finer types of yarn that the semi-automatic mules could not produce until further improvements had been made to them. The building of new mills for cotton spinning on the Arkwright system was severely checked and few seem to have been erected after the mid 1790s. Improvements to the water frame continued to be made however and it evolved into what was practically a new type of spinning machine that became known as the throstle. The throstle could produce certain types of yarn better than they could be produced on the mule and throstle spinning continued for many years, although on nothing like the scale of mule spinning.

Possibly the first powered mule spinning mills in Mottram or Hollingworth were those erected at Hill End and Hodge, both in Mottram township, but it is more likely that one or both was of some other type. Hill End Mill was built about 1794 on Hurst Clough Brook and Hodge Mill (not to be confused with the former woollen mill of the same name) about 1796 on the River Etherow. Otherwise, the first purpose-built mule spinning mill in the district would appear to have been Broadbottom Mill, which commenced working in 1803. It was founded by John Sidebottom and worked by his sons William and George. John Sidebottom had been working Millbrook Mill since 1789, a period during which a shrewd businessman, blessed with a certain amount of good fortune, could make large profits from cotton spinning and accrue a huge amount of capital. The site of the mill at Broadbottom, on the banks of the River Etherow, was a potentially excellent water power site provided that the substantial costs of the necessary works for realising that potential could be met. John Sidebottom was clearly up to the task and not only did he carry out those works but he built the largest cotton mill that had been erected in Mottram or Hollingworth up to that time, for spinning cotton by a mixture of mules and throstles.

Of the dozen or so water powered cotton mills that were active in Mottram and Hollingworth by 1800, about half had ceased to be used as cotton mills by the end of the Napoleonic Wars in 1815. The copious amounts of pure water provided by the River Etherow caught the attention of calico printers at an early date. The old Hodge Mill site was converted to calico printing in 1805 by Samuel Matley of Manchester, and Thomas Cardwell sold Hollingworth Mill to the calico printer Thomas Dalton in 1802. The dislocation of trade due to the wars made survival as a mill owner particularly challenging and profitability in many cases was adversely affected by the locations of the mills. The majority of the early water powered mills in Mottram and

Hollingworth must have been established on small streams that could provide only a very limited amount of motive power. This limitation formed an effective barrier to the expansion of the mill. Also these streams were prone to running dry in the summer and to flooding at any time of year; in either case production was liable to be interrupted. A more regular flow of water to the water wheel could be obtained by the construction of a reservoir, where water could be stored overnight ready for use the next day, but this usually entailed the building of expensive earthworks. Another possible course of action was to install a steam engine, either for use when the flow of water was insufficient or to replace the water power system completely. In the latter case a sufficiently powerful steam engine might enable expansion of the factory.

The earliest known record of the use of a steam engine in a cotton mill in the district occurs in 1805, at Arrowscroft Mill, Hollingworth[4]. By that date water power seems to have been abandoned at the mill and motive power was being supplied by a 'nearly new' 16 hp steam engine. The owner of Arrowscroft Mill, Thomas Cardwell, was also involved in coal mining, at the Hague in Mottram. Coal mining in the area was never very extensive, and in 1809 there were just two other coal mines apart from Cardwell's, at the Mudd (Mottram Colliery) and at Broadbottom[5]. There is also a question mark as to the quality of the coal mined locally, due to Aikin's dismissive statement in 1795 that 'coals of an indifferent quality are occasionally got at Mottram'[6]. It would appear that the local coal was unsuitable for use as fuel for the engine boilers at Arrowscroft, for in 1805, when the factory was

advertised for sale, it was stated that coal was obtainable three miles away at threepence per cwt, or laid down at the mill at eightpence per cwt. It is likely that the source of the coal was one or more of the numerous mines in the Newton and Dukinfield district. Other early steam engines were installed at Hill End Mill, at Wood's Mill at Wednescough Green, where the engine seems to have replaced the water wheel, and at Millbrook Mill, where the engine was intended as a back-up for the two water wheels, for use in times of drought.

According to a House of Lords Report[7] the six cotton mills at 'Mottram', which must have included both Mottram and Hollingworth townships, employed 587 workers in 1818. This figure represents roughly one in five of the total population and the factory based cotton industry was plainly of great importance to the local economy. Hill End Mill closed down not long after 1818 and the number of active cotton mills in Mottram and Hollingworth, excluding the two print works on the River Etherow, was reduced to just four following the conversion of Wood's former mill at Wednescough Green, Hollingworth, to paper manufacturing around 1830. No new cotton mill sites had been developed in either township by the latter date after the opening of Broadbottom Mills in 1803 but nevertheless the cotton industry of the district did expand during that period. Large additions were made by members of the Sidebottom family to Broadbottom Mills in 1814-15 and 1824 which more than compensated for the mills, most of them very small, that had closed. This expansion though was modest compared to that which took place at other townships within a radius of a few miles. Between the censuses of

1801 and 1831 the population of Hollingworth increased from 910 to 1,760 and of Mottram from 948 to 2,144, healthy rates of increase that were no doubt mainly due to the developments in the local cotton spinning and calico printing industries. However, during the same period the populations of Hyde and Newton townships, which in 1801 were of similar size to those of Mottram and Hollingworth, each increased by a factor of about six! Probably the main factor inhibiting investment in the local cotton industry was the lack of locally mined coal of suitable quality. The district also lacked a canal, which would have greatly facilitated the transport of supplies of coal to the local mills. It has been mentioned above that the cost of transporting coal by road over a distance of about three miles to Arrowscroft Mill in 1805 almost tripled the price. The townships of Hyde and Newton had the great advantages that they contained numerous coal mines and the Peak Forest canal passed through both places.

Although power loom weaving was carried on in Hyde from as early as 1813 and in Stalybridge by 1817, it was not introduced into Mottram and Hollingworth until the 1830s. Power looms were first employed at Broadbottom and Millbrook Mills by the Sidebottoms about 1833 and at Arrowscroft Mill around 1835. Neither the Sidebottoms nor John Hollingworth at Arrowscroft Mill had previously been involved in cotton cloth manufacturing on the domestic system and, indeed, there is no indication that any other mill owners in the district had been or were involved. Neither is there any record of anyone else based in the district being in business for cotton cloth manufacturing on the domestic system. Nevertheless, the baptism records of Mottram parish church indicate that in the period 1819-1823 about one in nine fathers was a hand loom weaver in Mottram and Hollingworth townships. This proportion translates into a very approximate total for both townships of 230 hand loom weavers[8]. Presumably they were being employed by masters based outside the district. Some of the weavers were no doubt working on woollen cloths rather than cotton but they were probably few in number considering the apparently small size of the local woollen industry. Clothiers, small independent producers of woollen cloth, appear infrequently in the baptism records of the period, far less frequently than for Staley township and especially for Micklehurst. Also, just three small mills have been identified as probable woollen mills active in the early part of the nineteenth century; all three were located not far from Roe Cross and seem to have formed a small extension of the Staley woollen industry into the Mottram district.

It is probable that the number of cotton hand loom weavers fell rapidly after the introduction of power loom weaving into the district in the first half of the 1830s. By the time of the 1841 census there were almost certainly fewer than a hundred cotton hand loom weavers in Mottram and Hollingworth townships combined. The census enumerators unfortunately failed to differentiate between power loom weavers and hand loom weavers in many instances. Out of about 140 people described as 'weaver' or 'cotton weaver' about 40 were too old to have been likely power loom weavers and were therefore probably hand loom weavers, but it is probable that of the remainder only a small proportion were hand loom weavers.

For the 1851 census, more care was taken to distinguish between hand loom and power loom weavers in Hollingworth township. A total of 259 people were described as 'power loom weaver', another 18 simply as 'weaver' and only 9 as 'hand loom weaver'. It is clear that by mid century hand loom weaving was almost extinct at Hollingworth. Of the nine specified hand loom weavers, eight of whom were stated to be working on cotton, seven were over 40 years of age and the eldest was 83 years old. There is no reason to suppose that the situation at Mottram, where hand loom and power loom weavers again remained largely undifferentiated in the census, was significantly different to that at Hollingworth. Just four hand loom weavers are specifically recorded in Mottram township, two of whom were father and son aged 87 and 61 years!

The 1841 census gives the first indication of the extent of employment of local people in the cotton factories since the House of Lords report of 1819, although the figures are subject to some uncertainty due to the problem of undifferentiated weavers already mentioned. In Mottram township there were about 470 workers in cotton spinning and weaving mills and at Hollingworth about 350, with similar numbers of males and females in each case. These workers represent about 15 % of the total population, but in addition there were many working in the two local print works. At Mottram township, in which was located the works of Richard Matley at Hodge, by 1841 one of the largest in the country, there were some 244 workers. The vast majority, about 220, were male, which was typical of the industry as a whole. The small number of females employed were mostly engaged in sewing together pieces of cloth. At

Mottram, therefore, there were very nearly as many men employed in finishing as in the spinning and weaving mills. At Hollingworth, where the print works of Thomas and John Dalton was located, there were about 90 males and just 3 females employed in the finishing trades, reflecting the smaller size of their works compared to Matley's.

In the early 1840s there were still just the same four mills and two print works operating in the cotton industry of Hollingworth and Mottram that there had been in 1830. Broadbottom Mills remained much the largest concern and would have employed more people than the other three cotton mills put together. Broadbottom Mills, along with the mills at Millbrook and Arrowscroft, performed both cotton spinning and power loom weaving, only the small Hodge Mill concentrating solely on spinning. On aggregate, about one half of the motive power of the four mills was provided by water wheels and only Arrowscroft Mill was wholly steam powered. The necessity of transporting coal a distance of three miles or so into the district at considerable cost remained an effective deterrent to new mills being established and was probably hampering the expansion of the existing concerns.

The arrival of the railway revitalised the cotton industry in the Hollingworth and Broadbottom districts. The Sheffield, Ashton-under-Lyne and Manchester Railway received its Act of Incorporation in May 1837 and the line became operational between Manchester and Broadbottom during 1842, and then was opened through Hadfield to Woodhead in August 1844. At last, cheaper supplies of coal became available from the mines of Newton and Dukinfield, through which places the railway also passed. The whole of the route between Manchester and Sheffield was opened at the end of 1845 and after the Sheffield, Ashton and Manchester Railway became a part of the Manchester, Sheffield and Lincolnshire Railway in 1847, Longdendale benefited from links to ports on both east and west coasts, on the Mersey and the Humber.

The railway brought with it considerably increased levels of investment in the cotton industry at Hollingworth and Broadbottom over the following 20 years. Extensions were made to Arrowscroft Mill around the time that it was taken over by Thomas Rhodes, while the railway was still under construction. John Sidebottom, at Broadbottom Mills, purchased a large plot of land near to his mills in 1849 on which he proceeded to erect a very large weaving shed, to hold one thousand looms. During 1852-54 Thomas Rhodes expanded his business still further by building the first phase of Mersey Mills by

the side of the Etherow. This was the first new cotton mill to be built on a new site in either Hollingworth or Mottram townships for around half a century. The mill was located on the Hadfield side of the Etherow, but still within Hollingworth, adjoining a branch of the railway that served the extensive cotton mills at Waterside. At the end of the 1850s Wood's old mill at Wednescough Green was rebuilt and extended and a new weaving shed at Millbrook Mill probably belongs to the 1850s also.

Investment in mills and machinery led to a rapid increase in the workforce. At Mottram, largely due no doubt to developments at Broadbottom Mills, the number of cotton mill workers resident in the township more than doubled between 1841 and 1861, rising to about 750 in 1851 and then to 1,008 in 1861. Most of this increase would have been due to the expansion of power loom weaving, a labour intensive process employing mostly females. This is reflected in the fact that whereas in 1841

there were about equal numbers of mill workers of each gender, by 1851 there were three females to every two males. Mottram township became increasingly economically dependent upon the cotton mills and the proportion of the total population working in them doubled to 30% between 1841 and 1861.

At Hollingworth the trends were very similar to those at Mottram and by 1861 the composition of the resident workforce by gender and the proportion of the population working in the cotton mills were almost identical. However, the size of the workforce resident at Hollingworth remained smaller than at Mottram, rising to about 475 in 1851 and then to 639 in 1861. This was the case even though the majority of the mills lay within Hollingworth, due to the overwhelming size of Broadbottom Mills in Mottram township. The total number of cotton mill workers resident in the two townships was considerably less than the number who must have been employed in the local mills and it would appear that a sizeable proportion of the workers must have resided outside the area. This was to be expected, given the peripheral locations of the mills.

Two new cotton mills were erected early in the 1860s, both of them in the vicinity of Broadbottom. One of them was Limefield Mill, built by Henry Kelsall Marsland of Besthill Mill, Hadfield, for cotton spinning, although it may not have commenced operations for some years. The other was the small West End Mill, used for power loom weaving. With the completion of Limefield Mill the number of cotton mills at Mottram and Hollingworth rose to eight, consisting of four combined spinning and weaving

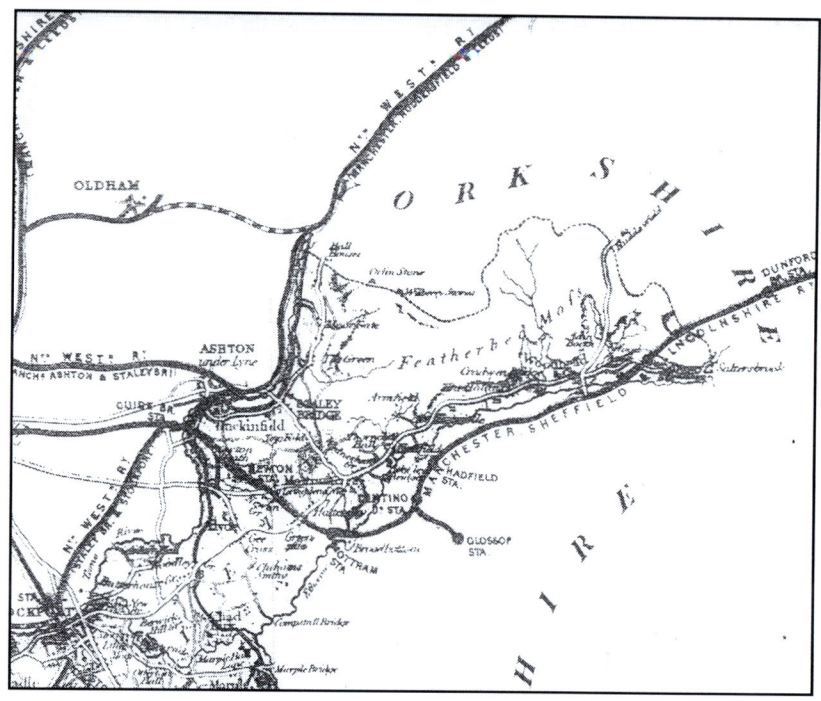

*Mid-nineteenth century map showing the course of the Manchester, Sheffield and Lincolnshire Railway. 'Mottram Station' is now Broadbottom Station.*

*Nineteenth century print showing the impressive viaduct carrying the railway across the valley of the Etherow at Broadbottom. In the background can be seen Besthill Mill, established on the Derbyshire side of the river in 1784 by Henry Kelsall, who was also connected with a mill at Hollingworth. From the 1860s until about 1889 Besthill Mill was run in conjunction with Limefield Mill, built by Henry Kelsall Marsland on the Mottram side of the Etherow.*

mills, two specialised spinning mills, and two small mills for cotton waste spinning and power loom weaving. The two calico print works, at Hodge and Hollingworth, were still in operation and still being run by members of the Matley and Dalton families respectively. There had been a modest degree of expansion in the previous 20 years at Hollingworth Print Works but at Hodge there appears to have been no further enlargement. Calico printing remained a major employer of local male labour and more than one in ten males resident in the townships of Mottram and Hollingworth in 1861 found employment in the industry.

The period of prosperity in the cotton industry at the start of the 1860s was brought to an end by a combination of the onset of one of the industry's cyclical depressions and the effects of the civil war in America, which commenced in April 1861. The depression was caused by the saturation of the markets for cotton goods while in America the blockading of the Confederate ports by the Union navy threatened to create a shortage of raw cotton. The subsequent period of poor trade and great hardship for the cotton workers later became known as the Cotton Famine or Cotton Panic.

In January 1862 it was reported that 'At Mottram and Broadbottom….the destitution is alleged to be overwhelming and the local help utterly insufficient'[9]. By the end of that month some of the mills about Hollingworth and Tintwistle were either stopped altogether or running only about one day per week. In the following August it was reported that 'In the neighbourhood of Mottram they were the first to feel the pressure, many large establishments being entirely closed, and they were nearly as badly off months ago as they are now'[10]. The existing Poor

Law system very soon became completely unable to cope with the mass unemployment and short time working. The necessity of entering the workhouse in order to obtain relief out of the poor rates was suspended, but the hated labour test was still applied. The stigma of picking oakum or breaking stones was considerable and the Guardians of the Poor were only approached by the cotton workers when all else had failed. At least the Guardians made the concession of meeting once a week at Mottram in order to determine cases recommended by the relieving officer, in recognition of its distance from Ashton, where cases were normally heard. In addition a room was found locally for doing the labour test of oakum picking. Fortunately there were other sources of sustenance available. Private benevolence played a part, and in May 1862 it was reported that Ralph Sidebottom of Millbrook Mill, which appears

*Operatives during the Cotton Famine waiting for their breakfast in the courtyard of Hill End House, Mottram, the residence of John Chapman.*

to have not been working, was giving out two loaves per week to each of his employees and providing breakfast each day for the children. Also, at the residence of a 'worthy lady' in the vicinity of Broadbottom more than 200 people were being sustained by her charity[11]. Another provider of sustenance was John Chapman of Hill End House, a large local landowner.

Local relief committees were formed all over the cotton districts that acted as recipients of donations of money, clothing, fuel and other items and saw to its distribution according to need. Such a committee would appear to have been in existence at Mottram by the end of May 1862 when the sum of £100 was given by the Mansion House fund in London to help relieve the situation in the district. In July a similar committee was formed covering Broadbottom and Charlesworth.

At the height of the distress, in January 1863, the Broadbottom and Charlesworth Relief Committee was giving financial support to over 400 families, consisting of nearly 1,800 individuals, at a weekly cost of just over £100[12]. The committee was also distributing large quantities of new and used clothing. Although the general situation in the cotton districts thereafter showed a gradual improvement, in the following April almost every man at Broadbottom was wholly unemployed and presumably the state of female employment was equally bad. The pressure on the funds of the local relief committee was great and it was deemed necessary to reduce the rate of relief given out per person. Many of the men in the district had been put to work repairing the roads as a condition of receiving relief, a common practice in the cotton districts aimed at preventing the

men from drifting into habitual idleness. When the cut in relief was made known the men refused to work at the reduced rate and it was reported by Mr Adamson, the visitor of the Manchester based Central Executive Committee to the various local committees, that 'the unemployed operatives had congregated in large numbers in the streets of Broadbottom, and that some fears of a riotous outbreak were entertained'[13]. Coming so soon after the serious rioting at nearby Stalybridge and adjacent towns in the previous month, Mr Adamson's fears were no doubt very real. There was clearly a degree of distrust by the men of at least some members of the local committee and some ill feeling had developed. In the event, however, the men contented themselves with a protest march from Broadbottom to Charlesworth, after which, following some discussion, they agreed to work at the reduced rate.

Judging by the amounts of money granted to the local relief committees at Mottram and Broadbottom and Charlesworth by the Mansion House fund and the Central Executive Committee the numbers claiming relief in those districts started to decline from about the middle of 1863. However, at Broadbottom in particular, this reduction may have owed more to the migration of people out of the district looking for work than to any improvement in the working of the local mills. The death of John Sidebottom, sole owner of Broadbottom Mills, in June 1863, was a huge blow for the district and probably removed any hope that the mills might re-open in the near future. Also, Ralph Sidebottom of Millbrook Mills died in the same year and the mills probably closed permanently from that time. The local relief committees may have ceased operations in or shortly after June 1864. In the previous month the Board of Guardians considered giving up the room at Mottram

that had been used for performance of the labour test due to the reduced numbers attending. At the start of the year there had been just 17 unemployed factory workers picking oakum at Mottram, while another 22 were employed by the Guardians on repairing the roads.

The American civil war ended in April 1865 but it was some time before the supply of raw cotton was restored to its pre-war level and it was not until 1871 that production in the British cotton industry again equalled what it had been at the start of the conflict. At Hollingworth and Mottram it was not until 1871 that the largest concern in the district, at Broadbottom Mills, re-opened, under the firm of John Hirst & Son. Broadbottom had fared particularly badly, not only during the Cotton Famine but also in the years following. During the period of closure of Broadbottom Mills in the 1860s the worker's houses associated with the mills were almost uninhabited. Whole terraces were empty and boarded-

up and grass grew in the streets to the extent that they resembled pastures. Even as late as the 1871 census, out of 218 houses in the enumeration district that included Broadbottom, 95 were uninhabited. In the whole of Mottram township the population fell from 3,406 in 1861 to 2,590 in 1871 and the number of cotton factory workers resident there dropped from 1,008 to 539. The township of Hollingworth fared somewhat better than Mottram in the 1860s, probably mainly because the large Mersey Mills of Thomas Rhodes were kept working throughout the Cotton Famine. The total population changed little, from 2,155 to 2,280, as did the number of resident cotton factory workers, which stood at 639 in 1861 and 650 in 1871.

After the re-opening of Broadbottom Mills there were six active cotton mills at Hollingworth and Mottram. Broadbottom Mills were no longer the largest in the district and had been overtaken by

*Undated photograph of Broadbottom Mills viewed from the Derbyshire side of the River Etherow. The spinning mills are on the left of the picture and the large weaving shed, with the adjoining multi-storey warehouse, is on the right.*

Mersey Mills. The two concerns between them dominated the local industry. There were two medium sized cotton spinning mills, Albion Mill and Limefield Mill, and two small mills devoted to cotton waste spinning and power loom weaving, at Hodge and West End respectively. The numbers of residents employed in the two local print works showed a small decline overall between 1861 and 1871, with the slight rise in the number at Hollingworth, to 114, being more than offset by the fall at Mottram, to 195.

Until 1845 there were no limited liability companies of any type operating in the cotton industry and all the mills were run by private firms with unlimited liability. After 1845 the number of limited companies in the industry remained small until the boom in joint stock company formation in 1860 that was cut short by the Cotton Famine. This boom, and the others that followed during the nineteenth century, were strongly concentrated in the area around Oldham and the Mottram and Hollingworth district lay on the outer fringe of that area. It is not surprising therefore that the first, and only, flotation of a joint stock company in the cotton industry in either of those places did not take place until the peak of the second and greatest flotation boom, in 1874. This company was named the Hollingworth Spinning and Manufacturing Co Ltd, although, in the event, only cotton spinning was carried out, the proposed weaving shed never being built. The company was of the mill building type, the intention being to erect a new mill on the site of the redundant Arrowscroft Mill buildings. Only about one quarter of the public limited companies formed in the nineteenth century built their own mills, the remainder being turn over companies that took over existing

mills. Of the seven original subscribers to the new company, three had addresses in Mottram, three in Hollingworth and one in Newton, near Hyde. They came from a variety of occupations; manufacturing chemist, two agents, two yeomen, engraver and tape sizer. The company was reasonably successful and remained in existence at the new Arrowscroft Mill for almost 20 years after commencing operations in 1877.

Private firms began to react to the competition from the burgeoning number of public limited companies in the cotton industry by turning themselves into private limited companies. The advantages of doing so were very significant for the management and financing of large firms in the industry. The first private limiteds were formed in Manchester in 1864 and then spread quite slowly until the 1880s, when the pace accelerated. Locally, the first private limited company was the Longdendale Cotton Spinning Co Ltd, formed in 1875 to run the Albion Mill, Hollingworth. After the formation of Thomas Rhodes Ltd at Mersey Mills and John Hirst & Son Ltd at Broadbottom Mills, in 1883 and 1884 respectively, private limited companies dominated the local cotton industry. Such companies extended their influence in the area subsequently so that by 1899 only the tiny West End Mill at Broadbottom was not under their control. At the latter date, both of the local print works came under the control of the newly formed Calico Printers Association Ltd, a private combine.

Between 1873 and 1898 prices in the cotton industry fell continuously, leading to reduced profits. Smaller profits and reduced expectations of future profits among employers acted as a deterrent to capital investment

and, although the industry continued to expand it did so at a much slower rate than in earlier times. Locally there is little evidence of mill building or of expansion of productive capacity during the period, beyond the construction of Arrowscroft Mill. The number of spindles in the mills of Hollingworth and Mottram stood at about 217,000 in 1884 and remained close to that figure until after the turn of the century. Weaving fared better and the number of looms increased from 2,376 in 1884 to 2,826 in 1899. By 1884 the firms of Thomas Rhodes Ltd and John Hirst & Son Ltd controlled two-thirds of the spinning capacity and, of course, as the only firms doing power loom weaving in the area, the entirety of the looms.

The small cotton waste spinning mill at Hodge closed permanently during the severe depression in the cotton industry of the late 1870s. This mill remained wholly water powered throughout its existence but was not the last in the district to use water power. Three water wheels were still in use at Broadbottom Mills until about 1880, when they were replaced by water turbines.

A branch of the cotton industry new to the district, the manufacture of cotton wadding, was introduced at West End Mill in 1886 and in the following year at Spout Green, in an old building that had probably been built as a woollen mill.

By 1881 the resident workforce in the cotton mills at Mottram had, not surprisingly, increased greatly from the low level of 1871, following the re-opening of Broadbottom Mills. The figure of 723 (258 male, 465 female) was still far short of the pre-Cotton Famine number, although by 1891 it had increased to 907 (338 male, 569 female) before falling

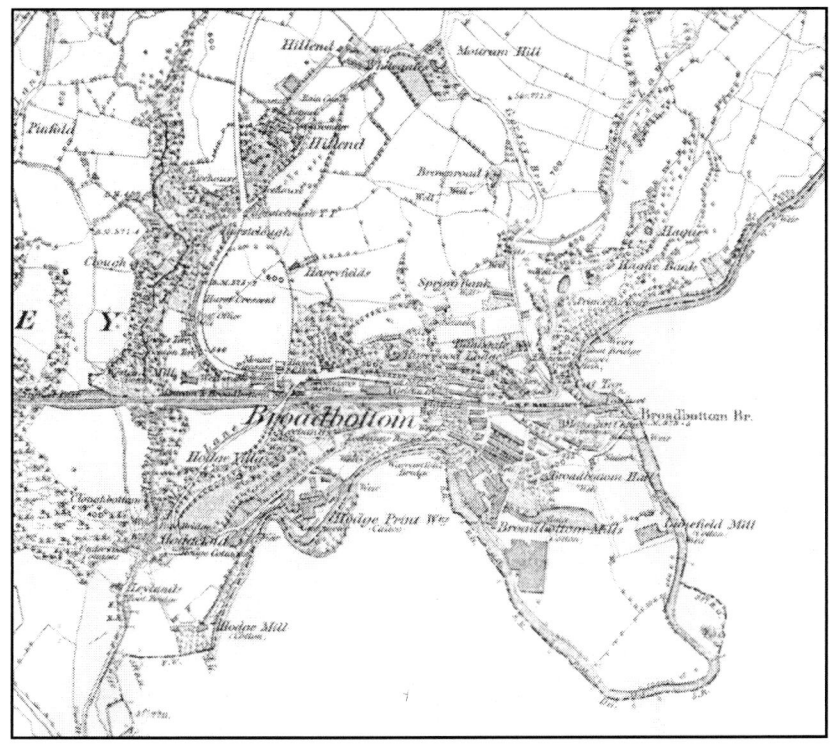

*Map of the Broadbottom district in 1872, showing Limefield and Broadbottom Mills, Hodge Print Works and Hodge Mill along the River Etherow and West End Mill on the northern side of the railway.*

back to 841 (296 male, 545 female) in 1901.

At Hollingworth, the resident workforce also increased considerably between 1871 and 1881, numbering at the latter date 860 (349 male, 511 female), due largely to the opening of the new Arrowscroft Mill in 1877, rising again to 1,001 (424 male, 577 female) by 1891. However, the extended closure of Arrowscroft Mill between 1896 and about 1902, together with the closure of Hollingworth Print Works (see below), caused considerable hardship. By the middle of 1898 a number of the inhabitants had left to seek work elsewhere and about 140 houses were empty at Hollingworth. It was reported in June 1901 that 'There is a gradual but sure migration of workpeople from this district [Hollingworth] to other towns. The building of new mills in Ashton, Oldham and Rochdale are (*sic*) keenly watched by operatives'[14]. As a result the resident cotton mill workforce fell to 722 (290 male, 432 female) by

the time of the 1901 census and the total population of Hollingworth declined from 2,895 in 1891 to 2,447 in 1901. Nevertheless, in terms of the proportion of the total population employed, Hollingworth (29%) and Mottram (27%) had the greatest degree of dependency on the cotton mills in 1901 of any of the local authority areas of Tameside.

The local textile finishing industry was changed beyond recognition soon after the turn of the century. Both of the local print works became a part of the Calico Printers Association on its formation in 1899 and both were closed. Shortly afterwards Hollingworth Print Works was demolished and a large new bleach works was erected on the site but at Hodge the plant and machinery were removed and the buildings left standing.

The English cotton industry experienced something of a revival between the turn of the century and the outbreak of the

First World War. There were several periods of high profitability, particularly during 1905-07 and 1912-13, which were accompanied by high levels of capital investment. Locally, investment was largely confined to Broadbottom Mills and Mersey Mills. At both locations the number of looms was increased while at Mersey Mills significant additions were also made to the spinning capacity. By the end of 1914 the aggregate spindleage of the mills at Hollingworth and Mottram had increased to about 236,000 and the number of looms to 3,444. Not all of the spindles were on mules, for ring spinning had been introduced at both Mersey Mills, in 1906, and at Broadbottom Mills, in 1904, where, by 1914, over one quarter of the spindles were rings. Ring spinning was a development of throstle spinning that was first introduced on a small scale into Tameside in the 1880s, although it did not become common until after 1900. Ring spinning was more productive per spindle than mule spinning but was considered suitable only for the coarser types of yarn, although it was gradually extended to finer counts[15]. By 1913 nearly one fifth of the total spindleage of the British cotton industry consisted of ring spindles.

One of the earliest uses of electricity for turning machinery in a Tameside cotton mill was at Mersey Mills, Hollingworth. In 1909 parts of the spinning and carding section of the mills were converted to electrical drive, utilising six motors. Electricity had started to be used in the power systems of Lancashire cotton mills in the 1890s but its rate of adoption before the First World War was slow. Mill owners were confronted by a wide range of firms in the electricity supply industry

*Photograph of Mersey Mills c1909, with the Waterside branch railway in the foreground..*

producing un-standardised items and many firms would not want the dual costs of scrapping and replacing up-to-date steam engine technology. The earliest conversion to electrical drive in a Tameside cotton mill took place at Droylsden in 1906. At Mersey Mills it was claimed that the regularity achieved by the electrical installation, which was by General Electric, was highly satisfactory and yarn production on the electrically driven machines was increased by 6%, besides the yarn produced being of a superior quality.

The problems that faced the cotton industry during the First World War doubtless affected Hollingworth and Mottram in a manner similar to the rest of the cotton districts. There was initially a labour shortage in the industry as large numbers of men joined the armed forces, which was mitigated by the recruitment of women to do many of the jobs that had formerly been a male preserve. However, as the war progressed imports of raw cotton were restricted due to the effects of the German submarine campaign and, with the inevitable decline in production, the demand for labour was reduced. The local factories were able to carry on working under the same ownership throughout the war, although it is likely that at any particular time a part of the machinery would not be in use.

After the end of the war there was a flood of orders for Lancashire cotton goods from markets that had been unable to fulfil their requirements elsewhere during the hostilities. Boom conditions prevailed in the Lancashire cotton industry and investment in buildings and machinery would have been heavy but for the fact that building contractors and engineering firms were in no position to supply the necessary materials and equipment. What happened instead was that many firms in the cotton industry were reconstituted or recapitalised at grossly inflated values as investors scrambled for a share of the huge profits that were to be made. Locally the only firm to undergo such a transformation was Broad Mills Ltd, of Broadbottom Mills and Limefield Mill, in 1920. In the same year this company was fortunate enough to find a firm that was in a position to convert Broadbottom Mills to electric drive, although at considerable expense.

During the First World War a number of countries took advantage of Lancashire's problems to develop cotton industries of their own, in particular India, which was Lancashire's most important export market. When the post-war boom came to an end in the latter part of 1920, due to the satiation of the pent-up demand for cotton goods, the new situation, in which Lancashire faced increased competition in its export markets, was fully felt for the first time. In February 1921 the position in the Longdendale Valley was reported to have worsened considerably. Nearly a dozen mills had been closed for periods of a week to 10 days[16], and the situation was similar throughout the cotton districts. The scene was set for what would be the norm throughout the 1920s, with the cotton workers struggling with reduced hours and temporary mill closures.

*The main block of Arrowscroft Mill, not long before it was destroyed by fire in 1982.*

At the time of the 1921 census, the number of resident textile workers, which included not only those working in the cotton mills but also those in the textile finishing trades, at Mottram had fallen to 710 (262 male, 448 female), while at Hollingworth it had fallen to 735 (351 male, 384 female). The comparable figures in 1901 had been 1,044 and 794 respectively. The total population of the district fell, but only slightly, during the same period. The fall in the number of textile workers since 1901 was despite the increases in productive capacity at the local mills and was doubtless due mainly to the radical changes that had taken place locally in textile finishing.

Initially it had been considered by many people that the predicament that the cotton industry found itself in was temporary and was similar to the numerous cyclical trade depressions that had always afflicted the trade. Later in the 1920s however it became widely accepted that the change was permanent and that the problems confronting the industry could only be solved by radical changes

to its size and structure. With no hope of any real improvement in the foreseeable future, investment in new mills and machinery almost dried up. Locally, only at Broadbottom Mills does any significant investment appear to have been made during the 1920s, in the form of the replacement of a large number of mules with ring frames.

With the arrival of the Great Depression trading conditions became even worse and in 1930 Broad Mills (1920) Ltd became one of the first local casualties of the cotton industry's decline. It was not at first apparent that the closure of the company's mills, Broadbottom and Limefield, was permanent but the eventual scrapping of the machinery extinguished any lingering hopes that they might re-open for cotton spinning and weaving. Similarly, Albion Mill, Hollingworth, ceased production about 1930 but the closure was not confirmed as being permanent until the machinery was scrapped a few years later. At the census of 1931, at Mottram 530 people (152 male, 378 female) were recorded as being textile workers, while at

Hollingworth the figure was 619 (266 male, 353 female), giving a total of 1,149 compared to 1,445 ten years earlier. Of course, only a fraction of those people would actually be working at any given time.

The hardest blow for the local cotton workers fell in 1933 with the closure of Mersey Mills. In February 1934 the chairman of Hollingworth Urban District Council declared the closure of Mersey Mills to be the biggest disaster to hit the area in living memory[17]. In the late 1920s the employment situation had been very bad, with one week's work in three being the norm at Hollingworth. By early 1934 almost three quarters of the local population was registered as unemployed and some people had not found a day's work in the previous three years[18]. In the following July it was reported that 'In the Hadfield and Longdendale Valley district things are in a deplorable state' and only the 'Co-op Mill' (Arrowscroft Mill) was working full time[19].

By 1935 the textile industry of Mottram and Hollingworth was represented only by Arrowscroft Mill, the River Etherow Bleach Works and a concern for the production of silk and rayon fabrics that had been set up in that year in a part of the weaving sheds of Mersey Mills. In April 1935 more than 60 % of cotton workers were unemployed in the Hadfield area, which included Hollingworth, Mottram, Broadbottom, Padfield and Tintwistle, and out of 2,000 members of the Weavers Association only 400 were in employment[20]. The power loom weaving of cotton had in fact disappeared in Hollingworth and Mottram with the cessation of Mersey Mills two years earlier. In addition, all of the spinners and cardroom workers were unemployed with the exception of those at Arrowscroft Mill, Hollingworth.

So far as the local cotton industry was concerned the period of the Second World War was most notable for the bringing back into use of Limefield Mill,

Broadbottom, where cotton doubling was carried on. The work at Limefield Mill was perhaps connected with the needs of the military but production was carried on there for some time after the end of the war.

In the immediate post-war period there was relative prosperity in the Lancashire cotton industry, for the same reasons as the boom conditions prevalent after the First World War. However, mill owners realised fully that the favourable conditions were only temporary and so investment in the industry was very limited. The inevitable downturn arrived in 1952 with the collapse of world demand for cotton goods. Exports fell, but also a new threat appeared in the form of rising imports of cotton goods into this country. The government made an attempt to help the struggling industry with the passing of the Cotton Industry Act of 1959. It was realised that despite the much reduced size of the industry, there was still much

surplus capacity and so financial inducements were made for the scrapping of old machinery, at the same time providing funds to help with re-equipment with up-to-date machinery. The occupiers of Limefield Mill appear to have taken advantage of the Cotton Industry Act to shut down the mill and scrap the machinery. On the other hand, J H Gartside & Co Ltd at Arrowscroft Mill probably took advantage of the re-equipment provisions to replace all of the old mules with ring frames over a period of a few years in the early 1960s.

Although there was some improvement in trading conditions in the years following the Cotton Industry Act, later in the 1960s decline set in once more, largely due to a fall in home demand. The sole remaining local cotton mill, Arrowscroft Mill, finally succumbed about 1969 when it was permanently closed by Gartside's and the Etherow Bleach Works closed about 1973.

## Notes and References

1. A valuation of the township of Hollingworth 1788. Cheshire Record Office DLT/D207.
2. Royal Commission on Employment of Children in Factories. First Report. D2. Evidence of Joseph Shepley. *Parl. Papers* 1833(XX)
3. J Aikin *A Description of the Country Thirty to Forty Miles Round Manchester* (1795) p458 [of Mottram] 'Within a small circuit of this neighbourhood there are twelve large cotton machines worked by water, besides a great number of smaller ones, turned by horses or small streams'.
4. To be sold or let. *Manchester Mercury* 16 April 1805.
5. M Nevell *Tameside 1700-1930* (1993) pp105-07.
6. J Aikin *A Description of the Country...* p473.
7. House of Lords Sessional Papers Vol CX 1819 (24) Appendix 32 Number of cotton mills and persons employed, by district.
8. The approximate figure of 230 has been derived following as closely as possible the method employed in G Timmins *The Last Shift* Appendix A1 pp211-22.
9. *Daily News* 18 January 1862. Commercial and Markets. Cotton Goods.
10. *Ashton Reporter* 16 August 1862. Meeting of Board of Guardians.
11. *Ashton Reporter* 10 May 1862. Meeting of Board of Guardians.
12. *Ashton Reporter* 24 January 1863.
13. *Birmingham Daily Post* 10 April 1863. *Ashton Reporter* 11 April 1863.
14. *Cotton Factory Times* 21 June 1901.
15. The count of a yarn is a measure of its fineness. It represents the number of hanks that can be spun from one pound weight of raw cotton, one hank being equal to an 840 yard length of the yarn. The larger the count, the finer is the yarn.
16. *Cotton Factory Times* 25 February 1921
17. *Cotton Factory Times* 16 February 1934
18. *Cotton Factory Times* 9 February 1934
19. *Cotton Factory Times* 27 July 1934
20. *Cotton Factory Times* 19 April 1935

# The Mills
# and
# Finishing Works

**Hollingworth Mill/Print Works**
Hollingworth Mill stood on the right bank of the River Etherow, on the site of the later print works, on the opposite side of the river to Mersey Mills. The mill was built about 1785 by Thomas Cardwell[1] and a valuation of 1788 shows it to have been four storeys in height, plus an attic; it was a relatively large structure, for the valuation is more than double that of the second most valuable of the seven cotton mills at Hollingworth at that time. The occupiers in 1788, and probably the original ones, were the partners Thomas Brown, Matthew Faulkner, Matthew Etchells and the owner Thomas Cardwell. They used the mill for spinning cotton twist using Arkwright-type machinery.

The partnership of Brown, Faulkner, Etchells and Cardwell was dissolved in June 1788, the business to be carried on by Matthew Etchells & Co, but by May 1789 Thomas Brown and Matthew Etchells, co-partners, were bankrupt. Although no more is heard of Messrs Brown, Faulkner and Etchells in connection with Hollingworth Mill it is interesting to note that they re-emerge very soon afterwards as the occupiers of the newly built Heyrod Mill, on the River Tame between Mossley and Stalybridge. Cardwell retained ownership of Hollingworth Mill and leased it to Francis Reynolds for 19 years from May 1789. Reynolds, however, only remained in occupation until 1802. The departure of Reynolds marked the end of cotton spinning at Hollingworth Mill, the vacant factory being purchased in 1803 by Thomas Dalton[2], who converted it for use as a calico print works. Dalton had previously been a partner in a calico printing firm with works at Manchester and at Shepley, in Auden-    shaw. Cardwell had previously attempted to dispose of the mill, in 1798, but was unsuccessful. The sale notice at that time mentions that the motive power was being provided by an 8 feet fall of the River Etherow, turning a water wheel 13 feet in diameter and 8 feet wide. The water wheel had been installed in the summer of 1797 as a replacement for an earlier one.

Only calico printing was carried out until the mid 1830s but subsequently bleaching and dyeing were also taken up. Thomas Dalton died in 1816 and the business was carried on by his sons, Thomas and John. In the following year, the brothers erected a new building on a part of the extensive site of the works, intended as a cotton spinning mill. The new mill, four storeys in height and measuring 92 feet by 31 feet, was turned by an iron water wheel 14 feet in diameter and 12 feet wide. Possibly this was a re-building of the original Hollingworth Mill. This new mill was advertised by the Dalton brothers for letting but they do not appear to have found a tenant and presumably the building was incorporated into their calico printing concern.

In 1840 Dalton's works contained thirty printing tables, used for block printing by hand, and five of the far more productive, but less versatile, roller printing machines[3]. Three years later the workforce numbered about one hundred, including sixteen boys and four girls under the age of thirteen[4]. At that time the works consisted of an irregular cluster of buildings of various shapes and sizes, by the side of the River Etherow. By the early 1870s significant alterations had been made to the buildings and this is consistent with the increasing size of the workforce during the period. The number of workers remained steady between 1843 and 1851, but then increased to 120 at the time of the 1861 census and then to 158 in 1871. Between the early 1870s and the end of the century little change appears to have taken place. Thomas and John Dalton continued to run the business in partnership until at least 1857 but John died in 1868 and by 1872 another John Dalton was running the business, employing 159 workers at the time of the 1881 census. The younger John Dalton continued to run Hollingworth Print Works until his death in 1895 and after that date the business was run by his executors for a few years.

On the 1st November 1899 Dalton's works formally changed hands and became the property of J H Gartside & Co Ltd. Almost immediately after the sale, the works briefly became part of the newly formed combine known as the Calico Printers Association before being closed. Gartsides then set about demolishing the old print works and in the first half of 1901 commenced the construction of a new works on the site, for bleaching (see River Etherow Bleach Works).

### Kelsall's Mill

This mill was in existence by 1786, when it was mentioned in the will of William Kelsall, where he refers to 'all my lands at Dog Kennels, wheels, engines therein...'[5]. 'Dog Kennels' is presumably a reference to Dog Kennel Fields, part of the Thornecliffe estate, especially as Thornecliffe Vale has a stream flowing through it, which could have provided the motive power; water privileges are mentioned in William Kelsall's will. Although William still owned the mill at the time of his death in 1796, his son, Henry, was given as the proprietor, in 1788, in a valuation of the cotton mills in Hollingworth township, and he was probably the person actually running the mill.

Henry Kelsall was the owner of the mill from 1796 until about 1823, along with nearby cottages. Until 1806 the property is described as 'cottages and cotton mill' in the land tax returns, and subsequently as 'cottages and mill', possibly indicating a change of use around 1806. About 1823 ownership passed to Jonathan Lee, who, in 1833, advertised the mill to be let, with immediate entry.

The mill consisted of three floors, each of 30 feet by 18 feet, and four floors, each of 18 feet by 15 feet, and there was 'sufficient water power attached'. There is no hint in the sale notice that the mill had recently been in use in the cotton industry or was considered suitable for such a purpose.

### Wagstaffe's Factory

In 1786 John Wagstaffe, a tenant farmer of Mottram, converted a barn standing on his land into a rudimentary cotton factory. It was located on the western side of Back Lane, immediately to the south of Old Post Office Farm[6]. Nothing is known of the type of machinery that Wagstaffe installed in the building or what sort of motive power was used to turn it. This factory may have been superseded by a small purpose-built cotton factory that John Wagstaffe erected close by (see Dry Mill) but it is possible that the two may have been run by Wagstaffe simultaneously.

### Hodge Mill/Print Works

Hodge Mill was in existence by 1763, when it was probably being used as a fulling mill[7]. It stood a short distance to the south west of the row of houses known as Summerbottom, near to the River Etherow at Broadbottom. About 1787 the building was converted for use as a cotton mill in the occupation of Neddy Holt, who about that time was also in occupation of Clough Mill on Hurst Clough Brook[8]. When Holt went bankrupt in 1788, his machinery at Hodge Mill for carding and twisting cotton, consisting of 'carding engines, roving billies and Dutch Wheels single and double' was put up for sale by auction[9]. A roving billy was a combination of the mule and the jenny, which was used for making carded cotton into rovings that could then be spun into yarn. Dutch wheels were ma-

chines containing a large number of spindles, perhaps about a hundred, used for twisting rather than spinning, cotton. They were in use in Lancashire by the 1770s. In 1789 the property was leased from the Tollemache estate by John Swindells, a cotton manufacturer of Hurst, near Ashton-under-Lyne, with Edward Moss and Strettie Seddon as sub-tenants[10]. Both Seddon and Moss appear to have left Hodge Mill by 1796, Moss building a new mill nearby. In 1799 Swindells took out a new lease for 32 years at an increased rent and it may have been at that time that he went into partnership with John Dale. Following the bankruptcy of Swindells and Dale the mill was let to Samuel and Joseph Walker. The Walkers dissolved their partnership at the end of 1803 when their lease still had two years to run and the mill, along with six cottages, was put up for sale in December 1803. At that time Hodge Mill was being turned by a water wheel that utilised a fall of 14 feet on the River Etherow. A mill race ran from a weir on the river through the middle of the mill, where a wheel pit was excavated in 1992. No details of the construction of the building are given in the sale notice but the 1992 excavations revealed that it was at least three storeys in height and measured about 36 feet by 68 feet.

Hodge Mill was bought by William Matley in 1805[11] but the occupiers from the following year are given in the land tax returns as Samuel Matley & Son. Samuel Matley was a calico printer at Redbank, near Scotland Bridge, Manchester, and calico printing was what Hodge Mill was used for henceforth. A doubling of the rental value between 1805 and 1809 may reflect extensions to the works and extra land was leased in 1818 and 1827. Purpose-built print works were erected near the

18

*The old-established method of bleaching cotton cloth involved exposing it in the open on a bleach croft for a period of two or three months. Croft breaking, the theft of cloth put out for bleaching, although a serious offence, was quite common. The use of bleach crofts steadily declined after the introduction of bleaching powder in 1799. The illustration is from* Cowdroy's Manchester Gazette *17 July 1813.*

site of the original mill in the early 1820s (there was a large increase in the land tax assessment between 1821 and 1822) and a set of three reservoirs on the north side of Hodge Lane are first mentioned in 1826. A gas works was added about 1834.

By 1840 Hodge Print Works was of a very considerable size. It contained no less than 221 printing tables, the second highest total for any firm in the country. However, the number of roller printing machines stood at six, which was about average[12].

Expansion of the print works appears to have come to an end by 1840 and comparison of plans of the site in sale catalogues of 1841 and 1919 reveal little change in the layout of the buildings. Richard Matley, Samuel's son, ran the business on his own account after the death of his father in 1829 and was employing 450 workers at the time of the 1851 census. He died in 1863 and the print works was advertised for letting two years later, when it was stated to be capable of printing 6-7,000 pieces per week and bleaching 9-10,000. A railway siding served the works and motive power was supplied by both steam and water.

Of Richard Matley's nine children, all of the sons and two of the daughters pre-deceased him and on his death the works was left to his two unmarried daughters. In 1870 the daughters sold the property (except for their nearby residence of Hodge Hall, built for Samuel Matley in the 1820s) to Ludwig Hamill. Hamill remained at Hodge only for a short time and about 1872 the Ledeboer brothers, Arnold and John, took up occupation. By 1887 there had been a further change of occupation, the new occupiers being Gibson & Costabadie (Milner Gibson and Henry Costabadie).

Hodge Print Works became part of the Calico Printers Association, a large combine formed in 1899, of which Gibson was a director, and the works were permanently closed in May 1901. The plant and machinery, which included 16 printing machines[13], was removed. The print works buildings were described as being 'in a wrecked condition' in 1917[14] and were demolished not long afterwards. The foundations and leat of the first mill on the site survive along with Hodge Cottage, a two-storey addition built onto the northern gable of the original mill.

One of the reservoirs is still visible and some stone-built dye vats, excavated in the 1980s, are on display.

**Clough Mill**
This mill was located at Clough, in what was formerly part of Hattersley, on the western side of Hurst Clough Brook. It was built by Neddy Holt, of Hattersley, in or shortly before 1788 when, along with an adjoining house, it was described as 'new erected'. The mill was of three storeys and measured 23 yards by 6 yards, with a cellar 9 yards in length, and there was also a wash house and store[15]. Neddy Holt also occupied Hodge Mill on the River Etherow. By July 1788 Holt had gone bankrupt and the cotton mill and house, along with a farm tenanted by Benjamin Mellor, were put up for sale by auction. The property was held under a lease for the lives of Hugh Holt, brother of Neddy, John Holt, Neddy's son, and Neddy Holt himself. The machinery in the mill was put up for sale separately, along with Holt's household furniture, and included cotton twisting, winding and warping machines.

In 1790-92 the owners were Neddy Holt's three assignees, Thomas Touchett, James Wardle and his son John but by 1793 the property had passed into the ownership of Isaac Worthington and the cotton mill was probably occupied by Joseph Turner. It is not known for how long Clough Mill was put to use in the cotton industry but it was probably not very long as there is no record of it after 1793. Joseph Turner later occupied a cotton mill at nearby Godley.

**Ashton's Mills**
These mills were in existence by 1788, when they were owned by John Ashton and his son

Samuel[16]. The property consisted of two small cotton mills, some cottages and a meadow in Hollingworth in the vicinity of Roe Cross. 'Cotton mills, cottages and croft' in the ownership of John Ashton & Son, until 1797, and then Samuel Ashton & Son until 1805, are recorded in the land tax returns. From 1806 only cottages and a croft are mentioned and the cotton mills had probably fallen into disuse.

Samuel Ashton of Roe Cross is remembered as one of the principal men involved with the building of a Wesleyan chapel at Mottram in 1791.

### George Kelsall's Mill
George Kelsall was the owner of a cotton mill, house and two cottages at Hollingworth in 1788[17]. Entries on the land tax returns for a cotton mill and cottages belonging to George Kelsall can be traced until 1803, but it is not possible to state the exact location of the property.

### James Harrop's Mill
James Harrop owned a cotton carding mill and cottages at Hollingworth in 1788[18] but it appears that later in the same year he relinquished ownership and the mill was converted to cottages. The exact location is unknown.

### Daniel Roberts' Mill
In 1788 a valuation was made of a cotton mill at Hollingworth belonging to Daniel Roberts[19]. Although the location is not given the mill probably stood on the site of the later Bents Mill, in the hamlet of Fields, off Green Lane, as Daniel Roberts lived at Fields. Roberts remained in occupation of the cotton mill until around 1799 and subsequently ownership passed to Mary Roberts. Entries for the mill in the land tax returns can be traced until 1812. By the time of the tithe apportionment in 1846 Daniel Roberts' old mill had ceased to exist, but by 1872 Bents

Mill had been erected at Fields. The occupiers of this mill were Henry and Robert Walker, engravers to calico printers, until at least 1879. In 1914 the firm of Henry Walker (Hollingworth) Ltd was in occupation, still for engraving. A 'mill dam' is indicated on the OS plan of 1906 and it seems likely that this dam was connected with the water power system for Daniel Roberts' mill.

### Wood's Mill
This mill was located on the site of the present day Albion Mill, on the north side of Wednescough Green, Hollingworth. In June 1786 William Wood took a lease for three lives from Rev John Hollinworth for the land that was to form the site of the mill, along with other land that included the site of three existing houses[20]. Wood's cotton mill was in course of erection in 1788 and appears to have been completed by the middle of 1790. The mill was stone-built and was powered by the waters of the nearby stream that flowed from the vicinity of Lumb, past the mill and then into the River Etherow a short distance down stream from Woolley Bridge. The reservoir, formed by damming the stream, that still exists on the western side of the site, may be original and was constructed to provide a regular flow of water to the water wheel. The nature of the machinery installed in Wood's new cotton mill is not known but it is probable that cotton was being spun there on the Arkwright system, using water frames.

When William Wood died in 1816 his sons, William and John, inherited the factory but the cotton spinning business seems to have been run principally by John, even before the death of his father, and he is named in trade directories from 1797 onwards. In the first half of the 1820s the cotton industry underwent an investment boom, which terminated abruptly

in the commercial crisis of 1825. Many mill owners suffered severe financial problems at this period and John and William Wood were among them. A commission of bankruptcy was issued against the brothers towards the end of 1826 and in the following May their cotton mill, together with the machinery, was put up for sale. In the sale notice the building was described as ' a compact cotton factory' with adjoining turner's and joiner's workshops and six cottages and a stable. The machinery included 26 carding engines, 15 mules of 204 spindles each and 23 mules of 192 spindles each, giving an aggregate of 7,476 spindles. The mule frames were adapted for spinning fine counts of twist yarns from 40s to 80s. There is no mention of a water wheel, although the reservoir is noted, and power was being supplied by a Bateman & Sherratt steam engine of 14-16 hp.

The property offered for sale in 1827 does not appear to have found a buyer and the mill remained in the ownership of the Woods' mortgagors, Messrs Jones and Roylance, for many years. According to the land tax returns for 1828 and 1829 the occupiers were Berry, Hill & Co, but the line of business of that firm is not known. By 1830 the buildings had been converted to a paper mill run by Samuel Oliver as a tenant of Jones & Roylance. Oliver is last recorded at Wood's old mill in 1850 and in 1851 the property was sold to John Warhurst by Jones, Roylance and others. It was probably used for a few years as a cotton waste warehouse until being re-built in the late 1850s (see Albion Mill).

### Millbrook Mills
The earliest part of Millbrook Mills was established in 1789[21], on the Tintwistle side of Hollingworth Brook, immediately upstream from where the main

Manchester road crossed the brook. The mill was water powered, the water wheel being fed by a long goit carrying water from Hollingworth Brook. After the death of the founder, John Sidebottom, in 1803, the mill was run by one of his six sons, James. By 1811 two other sons, William and George, were in partnership there as well as at Broadbottom Mills, trading as W & G Sidebottom. Millbrook Mill at that time contained about 6,000 mule spindles[22].

In 1816 an additional building was erected and a further, much larger, addition was made in 1832 on the east side of the turnpike road (Manchester Road), on the Hollingworth side of the brook. Power loom weaving was commenced soon after 1832 and there can be little doubt that it was carried on in the new building. The new addition was powered by a 20 hp steam engine while the older mills were primarily turned by two 10 hp water wheels, but backed-up by a 12 hp steam engine for use in times of drought. After the death of William Sidebottom in 1826 the firm continued to trade as W & G Sidebottom until around 1830, after which time it was run in the names of George and his nephew Ralph Sidebottom. After George died in 1843 Millbrook Mills were run by Ralph on his own account. In 1833 46s counts of yarn were being spun and in the later 1840s 30s to 40s counts and cloths known as shirtings and printers were being produced.

Ralph Sidebottom died in 1863 and if Millbrook Mills had not already closed due to the effects of the Cotton Famine they probably did so at that time. An attempt to let the unoccupied mills was made in 1871 but without success. The 'Old Mill' was described in the sale notice as being of four storeys plus an attic, measuring 74 feet by 24 feet, while the 'New Mill', undoubtedly the addition of 1832, was of two storeys plus an attic and measured 205 feet by 40 feet. There was by then also a weaving shed, containing 150 power looms, that had been built sometime 1845-63 and which measured 113 feet by 58 feet; this shed straddled Hollingworth Brook. In 1878 an unsuccessful attempt was made to sell Millbrook Mills and, after suffering a fire, the remaining disused buildings were demolished in 1882.

### Arrowscroft Mill (1)

Arrowscroft Mill stood just to the south of the section of the Manchester to Woodhead turnpike road known as Treacle Street, the present day Market Street, in Hollingworth. It was built about 1789[23] and the original owner and occupier was Thomas Cardwell, the owner of Hollingworth Mill on the River Etherow, not far away. Cardwell worked Arrowscroft Mill until about 1801 and then rented the premises to the partners Samuel Ousey and John Darbyshire. The partnership was dissolved in 1802 and the mill was empty by 1805. In April of the latter year Cardwell put Arrowscroft Mill up for sale or letting, with immediate entry. At that time the main building was of five storeys and measured just 47 feet by 37 feet. The motive power would originally have been provided by a water wheel turned by the waters of a stream that flowed down Thorncliffe Vale into the Etherow a short distance upstream from Woolley Bridge. By 1805, however, power was being supplied by a 'nearly new' 16 hp steam engine and there is no mention of a water wheel. The engine house measured 25 feet by 17 feet with two rooms above of the same size.

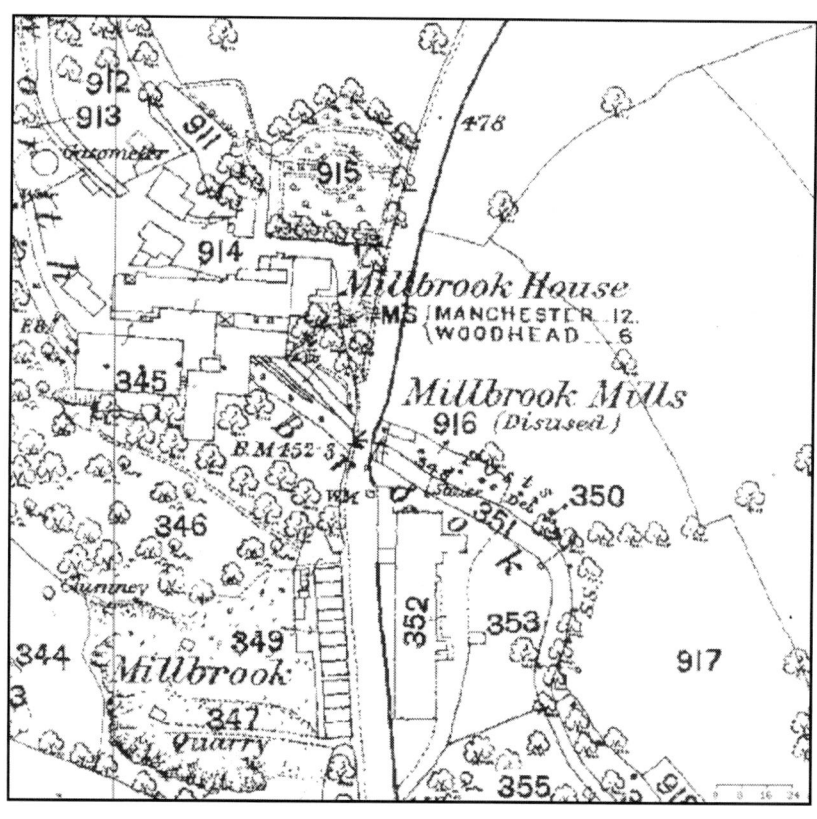

*Plan showing the disused Millbrook Mills c1872. The building numbered 352 is the large addition of 1832. Millbrook House was built by the founder of the mills, John Sidebottom; it was re-built in 1882 and still stands.*

> To Cotton Spinners, Manufacturers by Power, and others.— Sale of Valuable Machinery, part of it nearly new; for Preparing, Spinning, Winding, Warping, Dressing, and Weaving Cotton Goods; Tools, Implements, and Utensils. By J. DREW (by order of the proprietor, Mr. John Hollingworth, who is declining the business), on Wednesday, the 10th day of August, 1842, at the Cotton Mill, situate at Hollingsworth, near Mottram, in the county of Chester:
>
> THE Whole of the MACHINERY, consisting of one double scutch machine, 36 inches on the beater, by Crightons; one spreading machine, for 36 inches of wire, by ditto; eight breaking carding engines, 36 inches on the wire; one working roller, one clearer, 12 flats, wood-lap drums, in iron frames; three finishing carding engines, 36 inches on the wire; one working roller, one clearer, 12 flats, drawing head plungers, in iron frames; five finishing carding engines, 36 inches on the wire; one clearer, 14 flats, drawing head plungers, in iron frame; one composition grinding machine with eccentric motion; one composition grinding roller, for 36 inches of wire and fixings; two drawing frames, four double heads each; two slubbing frames, 20 spindles each, nine and a half inch bobbins; one ditto 30 ditto, one ditto 32 ditto, all by wheels, by Cocker and Higgins; one stretching frame, 72 spindles; one ditto 80 ditto, one pair of mules, 204 spindles, 16-inch rollers; one ditto 216 ditto, one ditto 240 ditto, one ditto 264 ditto, two ditto 276 ditto, 15½-inch rollers; one ditto 284 ditto, 16-inch rollers; one ditto 348 ditto, one ditto 368 ditto; one winding machine, for 60 bobbins of four inches; one 9-9 warping machine and creel, two 7-8 dressing machine, 42 7-8 calico power looms, making-up press for 5 and 10-pound bundles; cans, skips, driving straps, 9½-inch slubbing bobbins, 4-inch winding ditto; sough apparatus, warehouse and counting-house fixtures, large pack cart, four-wheeled waggon, quantity of cannel for making gas, new and old wrought and cast iron, and other articles.
>
> Sale to commence at 10 o'clock; and, for further particulars, apply on the premises, or to the Auctioneer, 28, Pall Mall, Manchester.

*Notice for sale by auction of machinery, tools and utensils at Arrowscroft Mill, from* Manchester Guardian *30 July 1842.*

Arrowscroft Mill probably remained empty for five or six years until Cardwell succeeded in letting it to James Sidebottom, who appears to have purchased the factory from Cardwell about 1814. Sidebottom replaced the 16 hp engine by one of 33 hp in 1823 and remained in occupation for cotton spinning until his death about 1829. Subsequently the mill was run by Sidebottom's executors until being sold to John Hollingworth some two years later.

Hollingworth did not commence cotton spinning at Arrowscroft Mill until Christmas 1832, and then about three years later he also commenced power loom weaving. He retired from the business in 1842, a time of deep depression in the cotton trade, by which time the mill appears to have changed little in size since 1805. It was described in 1842 as 'a small compact cotton mill with warehouse, stables and gas works'. The spinning capacity amounted to just 4,400 spindles, on nine pairs of mule frames, and there were also 42 power looms. In 1845 the tithe apportionment describes the property as 'cotton factory, reservoirs, gas house, buildings etc'. From the appearance on the tithe map it is apparent that the premises had been extended considerably in the previous three years.

Thomas Rhodes took over Arrowscroft Mill as a tenant of John Hollingworth in or before 1845 for cotton spinning and the manufacture of printing cloths. During 1852-54 Rhodes built the first part of Mersey Mills by the side of the River Etherow, which he ran in conjunction with Arrowscroft Mill until sometime in the second half of the 1860s, after which he concentrated production at Mersey Mills. Arrowscroft Mill then stood empty until being demolished at the end of 1874 to make way for the new mill of the Hollingworth Cotton Spinning & Manufacturing Co Ltd.

**Roughfield Mill**

Roughfield Mill stood on the site of the telephone exchange and the adjoining houses fronting Stalybridge Road, in Mottram village. The mill was built in the early 1790s by Thomas and William Harrop, who held the property under two leases granted by William Tollemache dated 1 May 1790 and 1 March 1792. In August 1793 the mill, with a house adjoining, was stated to have 'been built but a short time'[24]. Besides the mill and house the site also included a part of 'Ruff Field'. This seems to be an unlikely water power site and the machinery may have been turned by a horse wheel. It was in 1793 that Thomas and William Harrop encountered financial difficulties, probably as a result of the disruption to trade caused by the outbreak of war with France, and the mill, house and land were put up for sale. The property was bought by John Sidebottom and from 1794 to about 1797 the cotton mill was let by him to James Shaw. After Shaw's departure the mill appears to have been unoccupied for a number of years, being described in the land tax returns from 1799 to 1806 as 'silent mill' or 'still mill'.

After 1806 nothing is known of the former cotton mill until the

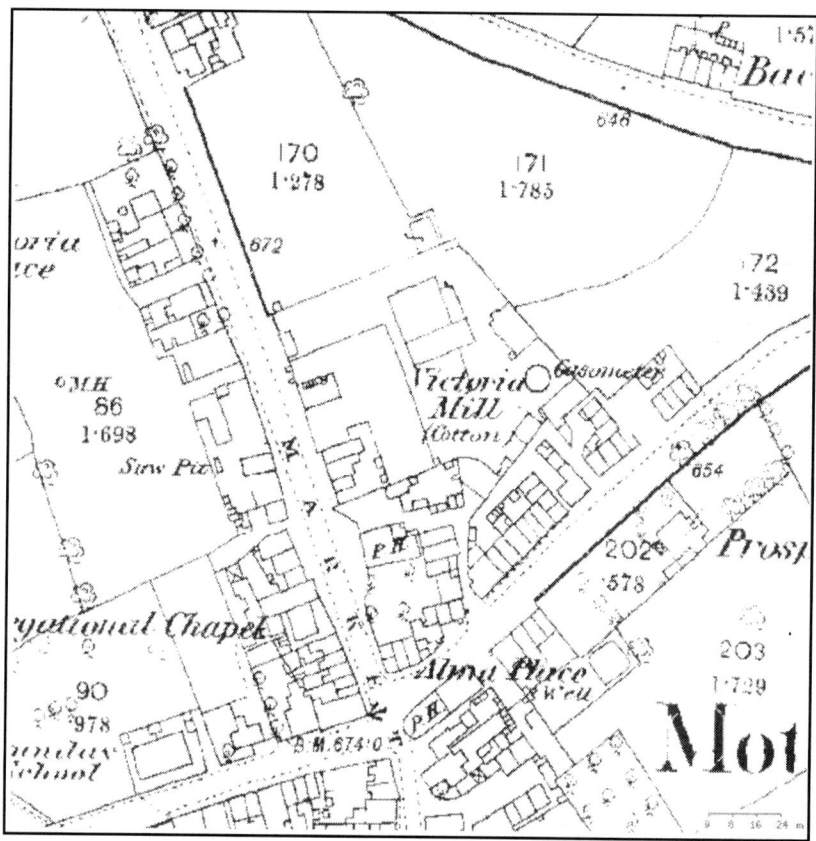

*Plan showing Victoria (Roughfield) Mill c1872.*

time of the tithe apportionment in 1847 when it was being used as a candle factory, in the ownership of Mary Cooper and William Henshaw. In 1856 William Earnshaw Cooper and David Cooper, trading as Cooper Bros, went bankrupt at the factory and by 1861 it had undergone a change of use and was again a cotton mill. The new occupiers were Bardsley, Leigh and Howarth, a firm of power loom weavers. The partners in this firm, Charles Bardsley, William Leigh and Robert Howarth, were all self-actor minders at Samuel Hibbert's factory in Hyde. Leigh, one of the founder members of Hyde Operative Spinners Association, and Howarth carried on working at Hibbert's factory, leaving the running of the steam powered 'Candle Mill' to Bardsley. Bardsley, Leigh and Howarth ceased trading in 1862. The factory re-opened in 1866 under the proprietorship of J Tinker and

in 1870, Albert Mill (as Roughfield Mill had become known) contained 167 power looms, along with twisting, winding and warping machinery. Three years later, however, the machinery was sold off and the factory (by then known as Victoria Mill) does not appear to have been used again in the cotton industry.

## Brittomley Mill

Brittomley Mill was located on the northern side of the main Stockport to Mottram road, the present Ashworth Lane, a short distance to the west of Hurst Clough Brook, placing it in what was then part of Hattersley township. The site, and perhaps the actual building, had been previously used for corn milling[25]. The earliest mention of a cotton mill occurs in the land tax returns for 1794, when the owner was James Cook and the occupier was John Holt, presumably the son of

Neddy Holt who had previously occupied another mill on Hurst Clough Brook (see Clough Mill). John Holt left Brittomley Mill in 1796 and the premises were still unoccupied when advertised for sale in 1803. The mill was described at the latter date as being stone-built and of three storeys and was of very modest dimensions, measuring only about 33 feet by 30 feet. Hurst Clough Brook was stated to be 'sufficient for turning, during the winter, as much machinery as the building will hold' but, in the summer 'the assistance of a steam engine would be necessary. And coals are gotten in the neighbourhood.'[26] The water power was clearly insufficient during dry summer weather, suggesting a possible reason for Holt's early departure and the fact that the mill remained empty for a long time.

By 1814 Brittomley Mill was owned by Isaac Gee and remained in his possession until his death about 1826. Gee let the property to a succession of tenants, including Thomas Harrison (1814), Edward Holdgate (1815-20), Daniel Wild (1822-23) and Thomas Wild (1825), none of whom had any known connection with the cotton trade. The mill was in ruins by the 1860s.

## Hill End Mill

This mill stood on the opposite side of Broadbottom Road from Hill End, close to Hurst Clough Brook, the waters of which provided the motive power. It is indicated on Stockdale's map of Mottram and its environs of 1794 and is first identifiable in the land tax returns of that year. Aiken describes it as being '…in a deep hollow, concealed from sight by an oak wood'[27]. The wood referred to was known as Flakefield (or Flaxfield) Wood.

The builder and original occupier of Hill End Mill, which in 1796 was described as being newly erected, was Thomas Lowe, son of Solomon Lowe who was the owner of the land and occupier of Whitegate House not far away. It was in 1796 that Thomas Lowe acquired the right to erect a weir across the brook and to cut goits to re-direct the flow of water, which was probably proving insufficient. The property was described as 'cotton mill and house' and Thomas Lowe was probably living there at that time.

Lowe went bankrupt in 1806 and by 1811 was letting Hill End Mill, first to William Burgess, then to Joseph Ingham (1813-14) and finally to James Harrison (1815-17). Thomas Lowe appears to have died in 1817 and early in the following year John Lowe, of Shepley Hall, Audenshaw, assigned the cotton mill in trust to James Antrobus Newton for Joseph and Thomas Sidebottom. The assignment included the '...mules, carding, spinning and roving machines...' in the mill and a steam engine had been installed by that date[28].

Hill End Mill remained in the ownership of the Sidebottoms until 1833 but there is no indication that the factory was used for cotton spinning for long after 1818. In 1833 the property, along with Whitegate House, was conveyed by James Side-bottom of Hollingworth, George Sidebottom, cotton manufacturer of Arnfield, and Joe Sidebottom, cotton manufacturer of Mottram, to John Kenyon Winterbottom of Heaton Norris. Hill End Mill was still in existence at the time of the tithe apportionment in 1845, when it was described as 'mill, cottages and yard' in the occupation of George Johnson and others.

## Hodge Mill

Hodge Mill was located a short distance to the east of Hodge Fold, by the side of the River Etherow, downstream from Hodge Print Works. The founders were Edward Moss, Robert Moss and Anthony Hardy, trading as Edward Moss & Co, and the mill was held on a 99 year lease from May 1796[29], although no entry for it can be traced on the land tax returns prior to 1799. The partnership of Edward Moss & Co was dissolved in 1805 and John Moss is listed as the occupier in trade directories in 1808 and 1811. In 1819 and 1820 the occupier was James Beckett, followed by Samuel Beckett from about 1821 until his bankruptcy 10 years later. A sale notice of 1833 describes Hodge Mill as being stone-built, of four storeys plus an attic, with the main building measuring 24 yards by 11 yards internally. Included with the mill was a house, some cottages, stables and a smithy. The motive power was supplied by the waters of the River Etherow, diverted via a mill race to a water wheel 12 feet in diameter and 9 feet wide, utilising a fall of the river of 9 feet. It was stated that the 'premises have never been prevented from working full time in the driest season'. No steam engine had been installed but it was mentioned that there was 'immediate proximity to coal' should one be installed. The water power system had been improved with the construction of a new mill race in 1805 and a new weir and race about 1815.

Hodge Mill was probably vacant at the time of the attempted sale by Edward Moss in 1833, but by 1836 it was being occupied for cotton spinning by William Kinder, although, like his predecessor Samuel Beckett, he went bankrupt in 1840. The vacant mill was again put up for sale, in 1841, by the representatives of Edward Moss and ownership passed to the Hyde cotton spinner Charles Howard. Howard let Hodge Mill, along with the machinery, to the Oldham cotton spinner James Radley in 1846. The machinery included four pairs of mule frames, with 540 spindles per mule, giving an aggregate spindleage of 4,320. Back in 1811 Hodge Mill had contained 4,292 mule spindles so evidently the mill had not altered significantly in the intervening years.

James Radley was still in occupation early in 1850 but he appears to have gone by 1855 when Hodge Mill was yet again offered for sale. The small dimensions of the mill rendered it unsuitable for the longer mule frames that were coming into general use and by 1855 all of the mules had been taken out and replaced by throstle and doubling frames. There was still no steam engine, but a new iron water wheel had been installed. The usable fall of the river had been increased to 14 feet 6 inches, presumably by further extension of the mill race, and the new wheel could produce about 20 hp. The next known tenant was John Jackson, who was in occupation in 1861 and combined hard waste spinning at Hodge Mill, on a couple of short mules, with farming. The workers at the mill, numbering just four men and four women in 1871, also worked on the farm and '...did anything between churning milk and packing cops. The blowing room man was Mr Sam Robinson (of Simmondley) and he also milked the cows and did general farm work'[30]. Jackson was still in occupation in 1878 but no record of the mill being used in the cotton industry after that date has been found. The building had been demolished by 1896.

## Dry Mill

This factory was built by John Wagstaffe on land opposite to the barn that he had converted to a cotton factory in 1786 (see Wagstaffe's Factory ). Known as Dry Mill, presumably a reference to its lack of water power, it was described in 1804 as a 'new building and workshop lately erected'[31]. Dry Mill was probably in existence by about 1797, and certainly was by 1799, and the structure is still standing, being at present put to residential use; it is stone-built and of two storeys. Unfortunately the building gives us no clue as to whether a horse wheel was employed as a source of motive power. Also it is not known what type of machinery Wagstaffe was using.

A cotton mill belonging to John Wagstaffe is recorded in the land tax returns as late as 1811 but by 1813 Dry Mill had probably been converted to cottages.

## Broadbottom Mills

Broadbottom Mills were founded by John Sidebottom of Millbrook Mill and were worked by William and George Sidebottom, two of his six sons. The mills stood on the banks of the River Etherow at Broadbottom. The first attempt at building a mill on the site, which was purchased from John Bostock in 1800, proved disastrous, as the unfinished structure was badly damaged by a storm in 1801[32]. However, the mill was re-built and completed in the following year, commencing cotton spinning in 1803[33]. In 1811 the original mill contained about 10,000 mule spindles and 6,500 throstle spindles for the production of 50s counts of weft yarn and 30s counts of twist[34]. In 1814 a second spinning mill was built onto the end of the first, both blocks being stone-built and

of five storeys plus an attic. The eastern block was 14 windows in length and the western block 20 windows, but it is not known which one was the earlier. They were aligned parallel to the river, from which they were set back a short distance. The newer block commenced production in 1815.

A third large spinning block was erected in 1824, a short distance to the east of the earlier mills and lying at an angle to them. Perhaps due to the commercial crisis of 1825 and the subsequent recession in the cotton trade, this mill was not got to work until 1827. All three mills were primarily water powered. The mill race appears to have taken water from the River Etherow from a point just downstream from Broadbottom Bridge, where a weir was built, the water then passing through a tunnel before discharging into a reservoir to the east of the mills. The water was then directed underneath all three spinning blocks before being returned to the river at the west end of the site. By 1833 the water wheels had been supplemented by a steam engine, for use during times of shortage of water.

All of the above mentioned building work was carried out by the Sidebottoms. James and Joe Sidebottom had joined William and George in the running of Broadbottom Mills by the 1820s, the firm then trading as W & G Sidebottom & Co, a title that was retained until about 1830, even though William died in 1826 and James left in 1828. The firm had become known as G & J Sidebottom by the early 1830s and continued trading under that style for many years after the death of George in 1843. After George's death, Joe took his son, John, into a partnership that lasted until the start of 1848, leaving John in sole control of Broadbottom Mills at its dissolution. In the later 1840s medium counts of yarn, up to 60s,

were being spun by the firm for the manufacture of cloths known as printers and shirtings, power loom weaving having been commenced in 1833 or 1834.

In the early 1840s the Sheffield, Ashton-under-Lyne and Manchester Railway Company built a railway line that connected Broadbottom with Manchester, before being opened through to Sheffield in 1845. The line passed close to Broadbottom Mills with a station at Broadbottom and this development was presumably welcomed by the Sidebottoms. In 1849 John Sidebottom purchased a large plot of land from the Bostock family by the side of the Etherow, to the east of his mills, on which he set about erecting a large weaving shed to accommodate one thousand power looms. This shed, in later years known locally as the Big Shed, probably commenced operations in 1851 or 1852.

The aggregate water and steam power of Broadbottom Mills, even before the erection of the Big Shed, was put at 240 hp and this was supplemented by a pair of steam engines of 120 hp when the new weaving shed opened. The long narrow shed, which may have been used for weaving, lying between the two earliest spinning blocks and the river, was probably also built in the 1850s. A large three-storey building adjoining the Big Shed, some 20 windows in length, was probably used for processes ancillary to weaving, and also for warehousing.

By the time that Broadbottom Mills closed in the early 1860s due to the effects of the Cotton Famine, compounded by the death of John Sidebottom in June 1863, they contained some 84,338 mule and throstle spindles and 1,646 power looms. The aggregate motive power amounted to about 400 hp, 130 hp of which

*Photograph of Broadbottom Mills, with the River Etherow in the foreground (no date).*

was supplied by three water wheels and the remainder by steam. About 1,200 workpeople were normally employed, making Broadbottom Mills by far the largest cotton mills in either Mottram or Hollingworth. The closure of the mills spelt disaster for the considerable community that had grown up in their vicinity and the great majority of the people had no choice but to move away in search of jobs elsewhere. Most of the cottages stood empty for years and grass grew in the streets of the once thriving settlement.

At last, in 1871, Broadbottom Mills were sold to the firm of John Hirst & Son by Alfred Kershaw Sidebottom, to whom ownership had passed after the death of his elder brother John. The Hirsts were woollen manufacturers and merchants of Dobcross, Saddleworth, who diversified into cotton with their acquisition of Broadbot-

tom Mills. The mills were operated at well below their previous capacity, but remained a sizeable concern and in 1884 60,000 spindles and 850 looms were in place. Coarse counts of twist yarn were being spun and printers and shirtings remained the principal cloths being produced. The power system was modernised about 1880. The three old water wheels were replaced with water turbines, the out-dated steam engines were modified and a rope drive was installed. It was said that prior to the installation of the rope drive the noise of the gearing and upright shafting could be heard 500 yards from the mill and that inside the buildings the noise was deafening[35].

In 1884 a private limited company was formed, the Broadbottom Mills Co Ltd, with Joshua Hirst as managing director. The productive capacity of the mills remained

more or less unchanged until after the turn of the century, apart from an increase in the number of looms to 1,197 about 1887. There was a further change in proprietorship early in 1904 when Broadbottom Mills were taken over by a group of Farnworth businessmen who formed the Broad Mills Co Ltd. Ring spinning was then introduced besides mule spinning but the company carried on with the same products as their predecessors, which by then included 40s counts of weft as well as 32s counts of twist yarns. The proportion of ring spindles was gradually increased and by 1914 the mills contained 45,326 mule spindles and 18,660 ring spindles. The loomage was increased and by 1908 stood at 1,442, still producing printers and shirtings. In the post-war boom the company was reconstructed as Broad Mills (1920) Ltd and also at that time the motive power was changed from steam to electric at a cost of about £80,000. Spinning capacity was increased to 52,832 mule and 27,236 ring spindles by the end of 1919.

Unusually, in 1929, when the cotton industry was in a very depressed state, there is evidence of significant investment in machinery by Broad Mills (1920) Ltd. There was some reduction in mule spinning capacity, to about 46,000 spindles, but the number of ring spindles increased to 36,700. The number of looms was reduced to 1,037. It may have been the case that these changes were part of a concerted effort to keep the business afloat but if that was the case it failed miserably. Broad Mills closed down in 1930 and never re-opened as a cotton factory. It was not until 1937 that the weaving and preparation machinery was put up for sale, so dispelling any lingering hopes that the mills would be re-opened by the Broad Mills Co Ltd. This calamity for the people of Broadbottom was mitigated somewhat when, in 1937, the Wilstand Manufacturing Co bought part of the mills and commenced the production of Axminster carpets and rugs. This company, however, ceased operations during the Second World War.

The mill buildings remained standing until serious fire damage led to their demolition in 1949. The site was purchased in the 1980s by Tameside MBC and a programme of conservation was initiated. Elements of the extensive water power system can now be viewed by the public, along with traces of an engine house, gas holder and various other buildings.

## Roe Cross Mill

Roe Cross Mill was in existence by 1830 and was probably built as a woollen mill. It stood on the site of the present Old Mill Farm, off Edge Lane and about 200 yards from its junction with Roe Cross Road. The change of use to cotton may have come about as early as 1834, when Luke Broadbent was a cotton warp manufacturer at Roe Cross. Certainly, in 1851 William Kelsall, a cotton dealer, was using Roe Cross Mill, presumably as a raw cotton warehouse. By that date a steam engine had been installed and the water power system was still operational.

After the departure of Kelsall, Roe Cross Mill was put to use by John Weston for the extraction of dye-wood liquors. When Weston went bankrupt in 1857 his equipment, which included a copper still and a logwood rasp, was put up for sale. At that time the motive power was provided by an iron water wheel and two steam engines, giving an aggregate of 22 hp. The water was directed to the water wheel via a wooden culvert 248 feet in length. The mill was offered for letting along with 'a good dwelling house', three smaller houses and stabling and with the option of a farm house and land. The owner was John Robert Hull, of Mottram Old Road. By the early part of 1859 the premises had been let to William Hague for use as a bleach works. However, Hague's stay was very brief and by August of the same year the mill had been let to William John Taylor, still for bleaching.

Nothing further is heard of Roe Cross Mill after 1859 and it may have fallen into disuse soon afterwards.

## Mersey Mills

Mersey Mills were located in a small part of Hollingworth township that lay on the Hadfield side of the River Etherow, between a branch of the railway leading to Waterside and the river, off Woolley Bridge Road.

The first part of the mills was built by Thomas Rhodes, proprietor of Arrowscroft Mill, during 1852-54. This original mill consisted of a stone-built five-storey spinning block with a weaving shed adjoining. By 1872 the mills comprised two large, five-storey spinning blocks at right angles to each other, along two sides of extensive weaving sheds. It is likely that the second spinning block was added and the weaving sheds extended around the time that Arrowscroft Mill was vacated, in the latter part of the 1860s. As a result of these large additions the workforce at Mersey Mills stood at 1,250 by the time of the 1871 census.

Thomas Rhodes continued to run Mersey Mills until his death in 1883, the business subsequently being run by a private company, Thomas Rhodes Ltd, led by two of his sons, Herbert and George Wood Rhodes. The eldest son, William Shepley Rhodes, ran Hadfield Mills that had been acquired in 1874, trading as Thomas Rhodes & Son. The latter mill became known as Rhodes Top Mill while Mersey Mills became Rhodes Bottom Mill. Around the time of Thomas's death Mersey Mills contained 81,000 mule spindles, for spinning coarse counts of yarn, and 1,526 looms, employed in the manufacture of grey printers, shirtings, twills and umbrella cloths, while the workforce had been reduced to 1,100.

The first major innovation by the new company was the installation of electric lighting, in 1887, to replace the old gas lamps. In the same year a new engine was installed, of 250 hp, made by J & E Arnfield of New Mills. It is clear from the OS plan surveyed in 1872 that the walls of the weaving shed on its southern side followed the curve of the boundary line between

## MOTTRAM.

FATAL ACCIDENT.—On Wednesday last, an inquest was held at the Organ Inn, Hollingworth, before Mr. Hudson, on the body of John Stott, aged 36 years, a labourer. The deceased had been working about 16 months at a new mill in course of erection for Mr. Thomas Rhodes, in Hollingworth, and was engaged on the previous day, with two joiners, running a beam along the scaffolding to its destination, when he must have missed his step from the side of the scaffold, and fell from the fourth floor to the basement, whereby he received such injuries that he died in about four hours and a half. Verdict, "Accidental death."

Manchester Times *17 September 1853*

Hollingworth and Hadfield. Later, however, the weaving shed was 'squared off' and the boundary ignored, presumably following the acquisition of extra land on the Hadfield side. This was done in 1887 when a small extension was built onto the weaving sheds, increasing capacity to 1,633 looms.

Further alterations were made to the power system in 1897, when another engine, in a new engine house, was added. This engine was a vertical triple expansion type made by John Musgrave & Son, of 825 hp; it appears to have replaced the Arnfield engine and another engine of 476 hp. It was supplemented by two older engines, a four cylinder compound beam engine of 627 hp and a compound horizontal engine of 393 hp. The productive capacity remained more or less unchanged until after the turn of

the century but there was some diversification into spinning finer counts of yarn, up to 80s, besides the coarser counts. The cloth being produced still included printers and shirtings along with twills.

The weaving sheds were further extended in 1902, thereby increasing the capacity by 120 looms, and considerable alterations and additions were made during the boom year of 1906. Virtually the whole of the mule frames, holding about 72,000 out of the total of 81,000 spindles, and all of the cardroom machinery, were renewed and ring spindles, to the number of 5,928, were added. The number of looms was further increased to 1,855. The power system was again altered, the two oldest engines being replaced by a single new engine in a new engine house; this engine was

*Photograph of Mersey Mills (post-1913). A part of the building later known as Longdendale Works, forming part of the River Etherow Bleach Works, can be seen on the left of the picture.*

> **Thomas Rhodes (1815-83)**
>
> Thomas Rhodes was born at Tintwistle on 13 April 1815, the son of William, a woollen manufacturer, and Sarah. In his youth he was a weaver but about the time of his marriage to Mary Shepley, the eldest daughter of William Shepley, a Hadfield mill owner, in 1837, he went into business on his own account. He started with just 12 looms in a part of his father-in-law's mill at Brookfield, the rest of the mill being run by his brother-in-law, William Shepley. Thomas's business appears to have prospered for in the early 1840s. he was able to take over Arrowscroft Mill in Hollingworth for cotton spinning and weaving and by 1851 his workforce numbered 250. In 1852 he commenced building the first part of Mersey Mills and by 1861 the total workforce at his two mills had grown to 700. The generally difficult trading conditions of the 1860s could not hold Thomas back and he greatly expanded the spinning and weaving capacity at Mersey Mills, probably at about the time that he closed the much smaller Arrowscroft Mill. In 1862 he built his residence known as Mersey Bank House, in Hadfield, where he lived for the rest of his days with his second wife, Amelia, whom he married about 1850, and his growing family. He continued to expand his cotton spinning and weaving business with the acquisition of Hadfield Mills, Padfield, in 1874, and by the time of his death nine years later he was running about 130,000 spindles and 3,000 looms and employing nearly 2,000 workers. Among his other business interests he was chairman of the Shireoaks Colliery Company, Nottinghamshire.
>
> In matters of religion Thomas Rhodes was a committed Congregationalist and a generous supporter of chapels at Tintwistle, Hadfield and Hollingworth. Politically he was a prominent leader of the local Liberals. He was also a Justice of the Peace, appointed to the Glossop Bench in 1857.
>
> Thomas died on 14 August 1883 after a prolonged illness and was interred in the family vault at the Independent Chapel, Tintwistle. He was survived by his widow, Amelia, four sons and four daughters, only the eldest son, William Shepley Rhodes, being from the first marriage. Thomas's personal estate was valued at upwards of £425,000.

another vertical triple expansion type, of 1,340 hp. The old geared transmission was replaced by a more efficient rope drive. Even after the installation of the rope drive, however, the transmission system was far from perfect and it was decided, in 1909, to adopt electrical driving for parts of the spinning section of the mills. The transmission was modified so that the engine installed in 1897 drove the weaving shed while the newer engine drove the spinning mill, partly by electric power; a three phase AC generator was driven by the engine along with the flywheel. The parts of the spinning section that were electrically driven were the twist cardroom, the spinning cellar, two spinning rooms and a frame room; three motors of 125 hp each, and three of 90 hp each, were employed. It was concluded, overall, with the changes to the motive power and machinery in the previous few years, that yarn production had been increased by 26% and coal consumption had been reduced from about 145 tons to 120 tons per week[36]. Further alterations and extensions at Mersey Mills, that were made in 1912-13 during the investment boom that preceded the outbreak of the First World War, resulted in the spindleage increasing to 99,348 and the number of looms to 2,002.

Despite the considerable investment that was made at Mersey Mills by Thomas Rhodes Ltd prior to the war, after the collapse of the post-war boom in 1920 the firm struggled. Like the other large combined firms in the Longdendale Valley, Thomas Rhodes Ltd was afflicted by periods of short time working and complete stoppages. Eventually the firm could continue no longer and the mills closed on 1 April 1930. The factory was taken over and restarted by the Lancashire Cotton Corporation in the following September but this was only a reprieve and production ceased permanently in 1933, when the machinery was disposed of. The multi-storey spinning blocks were sold off in 1936 and demolition was underway by November of that year and proceeded well into the following year. A portion of the weaving sheds was leased to a firm of local businessmen trading as Hadfield Silks Ltd, in 1935. This firm was quite enduring and remained in business for the production of silk and rayon fabrics at Mersey Mills until about 1969. Another part of the weaving sheds was used in the first half of the 1950s by Webbing Weavers (JG) Ltd.

The site of Mersey Mills is now covered by the Etherow Industrial Estate and little now remains of the old mill buildings. A long and narrow two-storey building, partly fronting onto Woolley Bridge Road, erected 1912-13, still stands and was probably used originally for winding. A single-storey building, of six bays with a north-light roof, is also extant and was also part of the 1912-13

*One of the few remaining parts of Mersey Mills; former winding rooms fronting Woolley Bridge Road added 1912-13 (photographed 2008).*

additions. This building formed the final addition to the extensive weaving sheds and stands at the eastern extremity of the site. The only other remaining building is located immediately upstream from a bridge over the River Etherow and backs onto the river.

It is a three-storey structure and may originally have been the counting house. The nearby bridge was built in the second half of the 1840s, presumably by the Daltons of Hollingworth Print Works, to give access to the newly built branch of the railway that served the mills at Waterside, Hadfield.

## Albion Mill

Albion Mill was built on the site of Wood's old mill at Wednescough Green, Hollingworth, in 1859, by the owner of the site since 1851, John Warhurst. The work may have been financed, at least in part, by Warhurst mortgaging the property to one Henry Thomas Darnton, an indenture of mortgage dated 5 November 1857 being made between the two parties, followed by an indenture of reconveyance from Darnton to Warhurst dated 26 March 1860[37]. The date '1859' can still be seen on a beam at the eastern end of Albion Mill. The original mill of 1859 was most likely only about half of the building that we see at the present time, for a dividing

*Abion Mill (photographed 1997).*

wall shown on a plan of 1879 indicates that the main part of the mill was probably built in two phases, being extended sometime in or before 1872. In 1875 Albion Mill was described as a modern mill, four storeys in height, measuring 200 feet by 48 feet internally. Motive power was provided by a pair of horizontal compound engines of 70 hp made by Wolstenholme & Rye of Oldham. Two residences, located between the factory and the reservoir, were probably built for members of the Wood family.

In 1860 John Warhurst was using Albion Mill for cotton waste spinning on his own account but by 1864 he was in partnership with James Hargrave. In 1872 Warhurst disposed of the mill to John Henry Warhurst of Ashton-under-Lyne and it may have been at that time that he also terminated his partnership with Hargrave. Certainly, by 1874 Hargrave was working Albion Mill on his own account for the production of 28s

to 36s counts of yarn, leasing the factory from John Henry Warhurst.

In 1875 there was a proposal to form a public limited company to be known as the Albion Mill Co Ltd, to acquire the mill from Warhurst as a going concern, for £18,650. The flotation of this company must have proved abortive for in September of the same year the mill was taken over by the Longdendale Cotton Spinning Co Ltd; this was a private limited company, one of the seven statutory subscribers being James Hargrave, the rest Bolton businessmen.

The Longdendale Cotton Spinning Co Ltd was short lived and ceased operations during the severe depression in the cotton trade of the late 1870s. Albion Mill probably then stood empty for several years but by 1883 had been taken over by J H Gartside & Co Ltd of Wellington Mills, Ashton-under- Lyne and Buckton Vale Works, Carrbrook; 40s to

44s counts of yarn were henceforth produced at the Hollingworth factory on about 25,000 mule spindles. Gartsides remained at Albion Mill until its closure as a cotton mill, with little change in products or spinning capacity. When the machinery was being scrapped in 1933 the mill had not been in operation for several years and the machinery in the bottom rooms had already been destroyed in the floods of the previous year.

Albion Mill was put to a variety of uses after the cessation of cotton spinning. The long term future of the building was assured with its conversion to apartments in 2002, although its external appearance has been somewhat altered.

## Limefield Mill

Limefield (or Lymefield) Mill stands a short distance to the west of the River Etherow and to the east of the former site of Broadbottom Mills. The mill was

*Limefield Mill (photographed 1997).*

built by Henry Kelsall Marsland of the firm of John Marsland & Bros, occupiers of Besthill Mill on the 'other side of the River Etherow, in Hadfield. Although built in 1861[38], the mill probably did not commence working until after the Cotton Famine and the earliest record of its use is an entry in a trade directory of 1872, when it was in the occupation of John Marsland & Bros, along with Besthill Mill. This firm was in the business of producing mule twist yarns for the home trade and the German, French, Russian and Indian markets in the 1870s and remained in occupation until about 1889. Subsequently Limefield Mill stood empty for about three years before being taken over by the firm of Edward Platt & Son of Hadfield. Platts became a private limited company in 1898 and in the early 1900s were carrying out cotton spinning and warping at Limefield Mill in conjunction with their Hadfield mill.

In 1906 there was another change of ownership when Broad Mills Ltd, who had taken over Broadbottom Mills in 1904, also took possession of Limefield Mill. Broad Mills Ltd produced 32s counts of twist yarns on 16,000 mule and 1,000 ring spindles at Limefield Mill and continued to run both mills until 1930. Afterwards Limefield Mill appears to have remained closed until some time during the Second World War. By 1944 cotton doubling was being carried out by Lymefield Mills Ltd, on 11,000 spindles, who were then succeeded, around 1948, by the Cairo Mill Doubling Co. The latter firm closed in or about 1959, having probably taken advantage of the provisions of the Cotton Industry Act. The principal aim of the Cotton Industry Act of 1959 was the elimination of surplus capacity, with the cost to firms of

scrapping machinery being borne by the government and by surviving firms. This was the end of the involvement of Limefield Mill with the cotton industry but the building has been used by a firm of screen printers for some years, thus ensuring its survival until the present time.

The buildings cannot have changed much in external appearance since being erected. The main block is, unusually, of three storeys, stone-built and is 14 windows in length and relatively wide. The original internal engine house is located at the south east corner of the main building, near the square chimney, and there is also a brick-built engine house. The latter was probably added to accommodate the new engine that was installed at the mill in 1904. A stone-built two-storey block, perhaps used as a warehouse, is also a later addition.

### West End Mill

West End Mill is located off Mottram Road, Broadbottom, just to the north of the railway and to the west of the station. The mill was built in or about 1861, the site having been leased by the

Tollemache estate for 999 years to Thomas Halstead in November of that year[39]. The original occupiers were Halstead Bros (Thomas and Jonathan Halstead), employing just 32 workers in power loom weaving at the time of the 1861 census and 38 in 1871; they remained in occupation until 1873.

The mill is still in existence and has probably changed little in external appearance since it was first erected. The main building is of two storeys plus an attic and also a semi-basement, due to the slope of the site. It is stone-built and eight bays in length, with a square chimney. There is also a brick-built two-storey warehouse that is presumably a later addition. The mill was out of use from 1873 until being let in March 1886 by Halsteads to William Flanagan, a cotton wadding manufacturer. Flanagan remained in occupation until his death and the mill was then worked by his brother until about 1899[40]. James Higginbottom, initially in partnership with a Mr Barnet, then took over for manufacturing candlewick, with just 260 spindles. By 1903, when the

*West End Mill (photographed 1997).*

occupiers were the brothers J & S Higginbottom, the capacity had been increased to 440 mule spindles, for making candlewick and torchwick, and also in occupation of this very small factory was Samuel Barrett, who was spinning cotton waste on 500 spindles. Barrett is not heard of after 1903 but J & S Higginbottom remained in business at West End Mill for a remarkably long time. By 1928 the firm had added the production of waste yarns to that of candlewick and torchwick. Although J & S Higginbottom continued to be listed in trade directories until 1937 it seems likely that West End Mill had not actually operated for some time prior to that date, as it was stated in 1935 that 'All the mills and workshops in Broadbottom have been closed down for a good many years'[41].

The departure of J & S Higginbottom marked the cessation of West End Mill so far as the cotton industry was concerned. The premises were subsequently used as a sawmill until the 1960s and afterwards, until the present time, by a woodworking company.

**Spout Green Mill**

Spout Green Mill was probably built for use in the woollen industry sometime prior to 1845. It stood close to a small stream at Spout Green, a short distance from Roe Cross on the road from Stalybridge to Mottram. The mill, stone-built, six windows in length and of three storeys plus an attic, is first recorded as being used in the cotton industry in 1864; in that year it was advertised for letting and was referred to as 'All that small cotton cleaning works'.

Spout Green Mill is next heard of again in 1887, when it was taken over by the Imperial Patent Wadding Co for the manufacture of cotton wadding. This firm, based

*Photograph of Spout Green Mill (undated).*

in Manchester, was probably attracted to Spout Green by the purity of the water supply. In November 1891 the Imperial Patent Wadding Co Ltd was registered to purchase the business from M. Brown-Westhead. By 1906 there had been a change of occupier and the Spout Green Wadding Co had moved into the mill, to be succeeded about two years later by the Spout Green Bleaching Co Ltd. No record has been found of Spout Green Mill being used subsequently in the cotton industry.

**Mottram Old Mill**

Mottram Old Mill was in existence by 1847 and was probably built as a woollen mill; it was certainly being used as a woollen mill by 1872. It was located in the fields to the south of Roe Cross Road, not far from Mottram village, with a reservoir on its northern side. By 1874 the mill was being used for bleaching by William Mason, who remained in occupation until 1877. This is the

last known use of the mill. In 1880 the vacant building was advertised for letting, along with a cottage and stable, but the property may have subsequently fallen into disuse. By the mid 1890s Mottram Old Mill was no longer in existence, although the reservoir remained.

**Arrowscroft Mill (2)**

The Hollingworth Spinning & Manufacturing Co Ltd, a public limited company with a nominal capital of £60,000 in £5 shares, was registered on 6 May 1874. The aim of the new company was to purchase the old, disused Arrowscroft Mill from John Hollingworth and to build a new cotton mill on the site. After demolition of the existing buildings, the first sod was ceremonially cut for building the new mill in February 1875. The building contractors were the Castle Hall Saw Mill Co of Stalybridge and the architect was John Wild of Oldham. Although it was originally intended to build a combined cotton spinning and weaving factory and plans to augment the share capital to allow for the construction of a weaving shed were announced in November 1875, in the event the mill that opened in June 1877 was for cotton spinning only and the projected weaving shed was never built. The new mill had cost about £15,000, excluding the machinery. The main block was of four storeys, was stone-built and held 34,000 mule spindles (22,000 for twist yarns and 12,000 for weft) on 30 mule frames on three floors. The remaining floor was filled with the preparation machinery, made by Curtis, Son & Co of Manchester, the mules being made by the Oldham firm of Asa Lees. The motive power was supplied by a pair of horizontal compound engines by Goodfellow of Hyde, rated at 800 hp, with geared transmission via a spur fly wheel weighing some 20 tons[42].

The Hollingworth Spinning & Manufacturing Co Ltd ran Arrowscroft Mill (or Co-operative Mill as it was commonly known locally) until the latter part of 1896 for the production of coarse counts of twist and weft yarns. In April 1898 the mill was put up for sale by auction and was purchased by J H Gartside & Co Ltd for just £6,000. It was then filled with machinery although it did not start production until about 1902. Gartsides had already taken over Albion Mill at Hollingworth and also ran factories at Ashton-under-Lyne and Carrbrook, Stalybridge. The new occupiers continued to produce coarse counts of twist and weft yarns at Arrowscroft Mill until just after the end of the Second World War, when the use of Egyptian cotton probably indicated a switch to the production of finer counts; the spinning of rayon commenced about the same time. A process of replacing mules by ring frames started around 1960 and was completed about three years later when all of the mules had been replaced by ring frames holding 10,360 spindles, rising to 15,160 spindles soon afterwards. Gartsides had probably taken advantage of the 25% re-equipment subsidy provision of the 1959 Cotton Industry Act, under which a total of 678,000 new ring spindles were installed nationally.

Despite these moves towards modernisation, Arrowscroft Mill was closed by Gartsides about 1969. The main spinning block was destroyed by fire in 1982, leaving just a two-storey building, about 11 bays long, on the northern side of the site; this building was demolished about 1986. The site is now covered by a housing development known as Highfield Gardens.

**River Etherow Bleach Works**
This large works was erected by J H Gartside & Co Ltd, both on the site of Hollingworth Print Works and on undeveloped land on the other side of the Etherow, to the west of Mersey Mills. Construction commenced in the first half of 1901 and by the latter part of 1902 a part of the premises had been fitted up and the machinery put to work[43]. The company in occupation was the River Etherow Bleaching Co Ltd, which had taken occupation of Bridge Mill, Hadfield, a vacant cotton mill, in 1901, before moving from there to the new works, taking much of the machinery with them. In 1906 the River Etherow Bleach Works had the capacity to process about 40 tons of heavy goods per day and had recently been sold by Gartsides to the Bleachers Association.

The River Etherow Bleaching Co Ltd remained in occupation of the works on the Cheshire side of the river until about 1973, but about 1949 the large single-storey building on the Derbyshire side, lying partly in Hollingworth and partly in Hadfield and known as Longdendale Works, was taken over by another firm of bleachers, John Walton of Glossop Ltd. This firm initially ran their newly acquired Hollingworth premises along with Charlestown Bleach Works in Glossop but two or three years later concentrated their business at Hollingworth. In the 1960s Waltons became a part of English Sewing Cotton Ltd and then of English Calico Ltd

*1930s aerial photograph showing Arrowscroft Mill*

and remained in occupation of Longdendale Works until the 1980s. Longdendale Works, which from 1974 lay wholly within Derbyshire due to boundary changes, no longer exists and a modern industrial building has been erected on the site, but parts of the old bleach works on the Cheshire side of the river are still standing

## Notes and References

1. Hollingworth land tax. An assessment for land that appears to have been the site of Hollingworth mill, owned by Thomas Cardwell, is identifiable from 1785. A house on the land was occupied by George Hollingworth.
2. J Graham 'The Chemistry of Calico Printing from 1790 to 1835 and History of Printworks in the Manchester District' (1846). Manuscript at Manchester Central Library.
3. G Turnbull *A History of the Calico Printing Industry of Great Britain* (1951). Appendix 2 List of English Calico Printers 1840.
4. Royal Commission on Children's Employment in Mines and Manufactures. Second Report (Manufactures). Appendix. *Parl.Papers* 1843 (430).
5. Copy of the will of Willam Kelsall, dated 1786 and proved 1796. Manchester Central Library archives M95 Chapman papers.
6. M Nevell *Tameside 1700-1930* (1993) pp60-61.
7. M Nevell *Tameside 1700-1930* p57.
8. Mottram land tax 1787.
9. Sale by auction. *Manchester Mercury* 2 September 1788.
10. M Nevell *Tameside 1700-1930* p58.
11. J Graham 'The Chemistry of Calico Printing…
12. G Turnbull *A History of the Calico Printing…* p426.
13. G Turnbull *A History of the Calico Printing…* Appendix 6.
14. *North Cheshire Herald* 5 April 1917. One of a series of articles detailing the recollections of the Broadbottom district of Wright Cooper, a former resident.
15. Sale by auction. *Manchester Mercury* 16 December 1788.
16. A valuation of the township of Hollingworth 1788. Cheshire Record Office DLT/D207.
17. A valuation of the township of Hollingworth 1788.
18. A valuation of the township of Hollingworth 1788.
19. A valuation of the township of Hollingworth 1788.
20. Deeds for Albion Mill. I am grateful to Mary Jessop for obtaining a copy of the deeds for my perusal.
21. Supplementary Report of the Factories Enquiry Commission Part 2 D1 Lancashire District.
22. Samuel Crompton's spindles census 1811.
23. Supplementary Report…
24. Sale by auction. *Manchester Mercury* 13 August 1793.
25. R B Robinson *Longdendale:historical and descriptive sketches of the two parishes of Mottram and Glossop.* (1863)
26. Sale by auction. *Manchester Mercury* 26 April 1803.
27. J Aikin *Description of the Country Thirty to Forty Miles Round Manchester* (1795) p464.
28. Assignment of two messuages, a cotton mill and land in Mottram-in-Longdendale, dated 13 February 1818. Manchester Central Library archives M95 Chapman papers.
29. Sale by auction. *Manchester Guardian* 27 July 1833.
30. *North Cheshire Herald* 5 April 1917.
31. M Nevell *Tameside 1700-1930* pp 60-61.
32. P Arrowsmith 'Broad Mills, Broadbottom. A 19th Century Cotton Mill Site in the Etherow Valley'. Archaeology North West No 4 Autumn/Winter 1992.
33. Supplementary Report…
34. Samuel Crompton's spindles census of 1811.
35. *Cotton Factory Times* 12 January 1934. Death of John Stringer, former chief engineer at Broadbottom Mills.
36. *Textile Recorder* 15 April 1910 Vol 27 p399.
37. Deeds for Albion Mill
38. J Bone 'History of Broadbottom' Unpublished typescript (1994).
39. Sale by auction. *Ashton Reporter* 23 March 1891.
40. *North Cheshire Herald* 5 April 1917.
41. *Cotton Factory Times* 31 May 1935.
42. *Ashton Reporter* 9 June 1877. Opening of Hollingworth Mill.
43. *Cotton Factory Times* 24 May 1901, 10 October 1902.

## Index of Mills and Finishing Works

## Index of Individuals and Firms

ISBN 978-0-9542171-3-6